Joe's Big Tables of Spanish Verb Tenses and Conjugations

The clearest, most logical, and best visual resource you can find!

By

Joe Kazemi

joekazemi777@gmail.com

Blank

Para Sundus y Maya, los grandes amores de mi vida

Blank

Preface

So, what makes these tables so unique and useful?

I have found that while many textbooks and websites that attempt to teach Spanish verb tenses and conjugations are wonderful resources, they tend to follow a traditional layout that is not conducive to real or rapid learning. They are not clear, logical, nor visual enough for my taste. They are neither engaging nor confidence-building. Nor are they mnemonic or pattern-revealing. They are simply not visual summaries!

No matter how complicated a subject matter is, it can and should always be presented through engaging visual summaries. That's what the human mind needs - and even craves - for real and rapid learning. And that's these tables are. When it comes to Spanish verb tenses and conjugations, they are the clearest, most logical, and best visual resource you can find. That's what makes them so unique and useful!

Thoughtful one-page "Big Picture" visual summaries have been my lifelong teaching philosophy as a statistician and data visualization specialist. I admit that I am not a native Spanish speaker (I'm learning Spanish as an adult to keep up with my kindergartener daughter, Maya, who is enrolled in a fabulous Dual Language English/Spanish program at our neighborhood public school in New York City's Upper West Side.) Interestingly, being a non-native Spanish speaker gave me an important advantage when developing these tables: Unlike many native Spanish instructors, I know firsthand what's it's like to be learning Spanish as a "second" language. I can relate...

With these tables, at a glance, learners can know which tenses and moods belong to beginner, intermediate, or advanced levels of Spanish. This is essential for planning and goal-setting. They can immediately see logical patterns through the consistent and methodical layout of the tables. They can almost instantly start forming sentences similar to the examples listed adding more vocabulary as needed. And they can work individually or in a team in a classroom setting where they would form a sentence and change its tense or pronoun at will to produce families of sentences. While they would probably have to peek at the tables to do so at first, it won't take them long before they can speak without peeking. Mastery of verb tenses and conjugations can be achieved with practice but only after sufficient levels of logic, confidence, and comfort are established. And once that mastery is coupled with a growing vocabulary, fluency is attained.

I have great respect and admiration for you, English-speaking adult learners of Spanish as a second language. Where I live, you are making my beloved United States of America, a richer and more beautiful country. Good luck in your endeavor to be fluent Spanish speakers.

¡Saludos!

Joe Kazemi
New York, NY
2011

Acknowledgements

I am grateful to my five-year daughter, Maya, for inspiring me to start learning Spanish in the first place and for my wife, Sundus, and niece and nephew, Ayat and Haydar, for encouraging me to follow through with it.

I am also grateful to a large number of friends and colleagues who have commented enthusiastically on earlier drafts of this work. They were a great source of support and validation, and their comments led to various improvements and refinements. I would like to thank Laith Yousif, Hilary Guberman, Mike Solomon, Anne Capelle, Jennifer Prada, Patty Frisbie, Ivan Guerra, JJ Arévalo, Ana Caceres, Kelly Nishimura, Elma Lorenzo-Blanco, and Raul Reynoso.

This could not have happened without each one of you.

Joe Kazemi
New York, NY
2011

Blank

Tres diferentes tipos de verbos en español

1. Verbos Regular (AR, ER, y IR)
La madre no cambia y las terminaciones siguen un patrón regular.

2. Verbos de Cambio de madre
Los cambios se derivan para facilitar la pronunciación, pero los finales siguen un patrón regular en ocasiones similares a los verbos regulares. Usted puede pensar en estos verbos como regular, "irregular regular", o simplemente irregular.

3. Verbos Irregular
Los cambios y las terminaciones de la madre no siguen un patrón regular.

Three different types of verbs in Spanish

1. Regular Verbs (AR, ER, and IR)
The stem does not change and the endings follow a regular pattern.

2. Stem-Changing Verbs
The stem changes for easier pronounciation but the endings follow a regular pattern sometimes similar to regular verbs. You can think of these verbs as regular, "regular irregular", or simply irregular.

3. Irregular Verbs
The stem changes and the endings do not follow a regular pattern.

Blank

Los verbos ***AR regulares*** *más utilizados en español*

Estos son algunos de los verbos AR regulares más utilizados regularmente en español. Con la ayuda de los tablas, intentar la formación de frases con sus diferentes tiempos y conjugaciones.

These are some of the most commonly used regular AR verbs in Spanish. With the aid of the tables, try forming sentenses using their different tenses and conjugations.

1 ***amar***	*to love*
2 ***andar***	*to walk*
3 ***aquilar***	*to rent*
4 ***ayudar***	*to help*
5 ***bailar***	*to dance*
6 ***buscar***	*to look for*
7 ***cambiar***	*to change*
8 ***caminar***	*to walk*
9 ***cantar***	*to sing*
10 ***cocinar***	*to cook*
11 ***comprar***	*to buy*
12 ***contestar***	*to answer*
13 ***dejar***	*to leave, to allow*
14 ***desear***	*to desire*
15 ***entrar***	*to enter*
16 ***enseñar***	*to teach*
17 ***enviar***	*to send*
18 ***escuchar***	*to listen to*
19 ***esperar***	*to wait, to hope*
20 ***estudiar***	*to study*
21 ***expresar***	*to express*
22 ***firmar***	*to sign*
23 ***ganar***	*to win, to earn*
24 ***gastar***	*to spend money*

Los verbos ***AR regulares*** *más utilizados en español*

★ 25 ***hablar***	*to speak*
26 ***lavar***	*to wash*
27 ***limpiar***	*to clean*
28 ***llamar***	*to call*
29 ***llegar***	*to arrive*
30 ***llevar***	*to wear, to carry*
31 ***llorar***	*to cry, to mourn*
32 ***mandar***	*to order*
33 ***marchar***	*to walk*
34 ***mirar***	*to watch, look*
35 ***montar***	*to climb*
36 ***nadar***	*to swim*
37 ***necesitar***	*to need*
38 ***olvidar***	*to forget*
39 ***pagar***	*to pay for*
40 ***parar***	*to stop*
41 ***pasar***	*to spend (time)*
42 ***practicar***	*to practice*
43 ***preguntar***	*to ask*
44 ***preparar***	*to prepare*
45 ***quedar***	*to stay*
46 ***regresar***	*to return*
47 ***saludar***	*to salute, to greet*
48 ***tirar***	*to pull, draw*

Los verbos ***AR regulares*** *más utilizados en español*

49 ***tocar***	*to touch, to play an instrument*
50 ***tomar***	*to take, drink*
51 ***trabajar***	*to work*
52 ***viajar***	*to travel*
53 ***visitar***	*to visit*
54	
55	
56	
57	
58	
59	
60	
61	
62	
63	
64	
65	
66	
67	
68	
69	
70	
71	
72	

Blank

Los verbos **ER regulares** *más utilizados en español*

Estos son algunos de los verbos ER regulares más utilizados regularmente en español. Con la ayuda de los tablas, intentar la formación de frases con sus diferentes tiempos y conjugaciones.

These are some of the most commonly used regular ER verbs in Spanish. With the aid of the tables, try forming sentenses using their different tenses and conjugations.

	1 ***aprender***	*to learn*
	2 ***barrer***	*to sweep*
	3 ***beber***	*to drink*
★	4 ***comer***	*to eat*
	5 ***comprender***	*to understand*
	6 ***correr***	*to run*
	7 ***creer***	*to believe*
	8 ***deber***	*to have to, to owe*
	9 ***esconder***	*to hide*
	10 ***leer***	*to read*
	11 ***meter***	*to put in, to insert*
	12 ***poseer***	*to possess, to own*
	13 ***prender***	*to catch, turn on*
	14 ***preparer***	*to prepare*
	15 ***prometer***	*to promise*
	16 ***romper***	*to break*
	17 ***temer***	*to fear, to dread*
	18 ***toser***	*to cough*
	19 ***vender***	*to sell*
	20	
	21	
	22	
	23	
	24	

Blank

Los verbos ***IR regulares*** *más utilizados en español*

Estos son algunos de los verbos IR regulares más utilizados regularmente en español. Con la ayuda de los tablas, intentar la formación de frases con sus diferentes tiempos y conjugaciones.

These are some of the most commonly used regular IR verbs in Spanish. With the aid of the tables, try forming sentenses using their different tenses and conjugations.

	1 ***abrir***	*to open*
	2 ***admitir***	*to admit*
	3 ***añadir***	*to add*
	4 ***asistir***	*to attend*
	5 ***cubrir***	*to cover*
	6 ***cumplir***	*to fulfill, to carry out*
	7 ***decidir***	*to decide*
	8 ***descubrir***	*to discover*
	9 ***describir***	*to describe*
	10 ***discutir***	*to discuss*
	11 ***escribir***	*to write*
	12 ***existir***	*to exist*
	13 ***interrumpir***	*to interrupt*
	14 ***ocurrir***	*to occur*
	15 ***omitir***	*to omit*
	16 ***partir***	*to leave, to divide*
	17 ***permitir***	*to permit*
	18 ***recibir***	*to receive*
	19 ***subir***	*to go up, to climb*
	20 ***sufrir***	*to suffer*
	21 ***unir***	*to unite*
★	22 ***vivir***	*to live*
	23	
	24	

Blank

How's any verb's big table organized?

Verb English translation

Beginner Spanish

Simple

Past

Preterite INDICATIVE		
I spoke		
Stem + Endings		
	Simple	Verb
Yo	---	
Tú		
Él/Ella/Usted		
Nosotros/as		
Vosotros/as		
Éllos/Ellas/Ustedes		
Example sentence in particular tense in Spanish		
Example sentence in particular tense in English		

Present

Present INDICATIVE		
I speak / I am speaking		
Stem + Endings		
	Simple	Verb
Yo	---	
Tú		
Él/Ella/Usted		
Nosotros/as		
Vosotros/as		
Éllos/Ellas/Ustedes		
Example sentence in particular tense in Spanish		
Example sentence in particular tense in English		

Imperfect

Imperfect INDICATIVE		
I used to speak		
Stem + Endings		
	Simple	Verb
Yo	---	
Tú		
Él/Ella/Usted		
Nosotros/as		
Vosotros/as		
Éllos/Ellas/Ustedes		
Example sentence in particular tense in Spanish		
Example sentence in particular tense in English		

Note: There exists also a "Preterite Perfect" tense (sometimes called "Past Anterior" which also means (I had spoken) using the auxiliary verb Haber (conjugated in past preterite tense - Hube, Hubiste, Hubo, Hubimos, Hubisteis, and Hubieron) + Past Participle. However, it is not used frequently enough to be listed here.

Intermediate Spanish

Perfect

Pluperfect INDICATIVE		
I had spoken		
Haber (Past Perfect) + Past Participle		
	Composite	PP
Yo	había	
Tú	habías	
Él/Ella/Usted	había	
Nosotros/as	habíamos	
Vosotros/as	habíais	
Éllos/Ellas/Ustedes	habían	
Example sentence in particular tense in Spanish		
Example sentence in particular tense in English		

Perfect Present INDICATIVE		
I have spoken		
Haber (Present) + Past Participle		
	Composite	PP
Yo	he	
Tú	has	
Él/Ella/Usted	ha	
Nosotros/as	hemos	
Vosotros/as	habéis	
Éllos/Ellas/Ustedes	han	
Example sentence in particular tense in Spanish		
Example sentence in particular tense in English		

Progressive

Progressive Imperfect INDICATIVE		
I was speaking		
Estar (Imperfect) + Gerund		
	Composite	Gerund
Yo	estaba	
Tú	estabas	
Él/Ella/Usted	estaba	
Nosotros/as	estábamos	
Vosotros/as	estabais	
Éllos/Ellas/Ustedes	estaban	
Example sentence in particular tense in Spanish		
Example sentence in particular tense in English		

Progressive Present INDICATIVE		
I am speaking		
Estar (Present) + Gerund		
	Composite	Gerund
Yo	estoy	
Tú	estás	
Él/Ella/Usted	está	
Nosotros/as	estamos	
Vosotros/as	estáis	
Éllos/Ellas/Ustedes	están	
Example sentence in particular tense in Spanish		
Example sentence in particular tense in English		

 joekazemi777@gmail.com

Future

Future — INDICATIVE

I will speak

Infinitive + Endings

	Simple	Verb
Yo	---	
Tú		
Él/Ella/Usted		
Nosotros/as		
Vosotros/as		
Éllos/Ellas/Ustedes		

Example sentence in particular tense in Spanish
Example sentence in particular tense in English

Near Future — INDICATIVE

I am going to speak

Ir (Present) + a + Infinitive

	Composite	Infinitive
Yo	voy a	
Tú	vas a	
Él/Ella/Usted	va a	
Nosotros/as	vamos a	
Vosotros/as	vais a	
Éllos/Ellas/Ustedes	van a	

Example sentence in particular tense in Spanish
Example sentence in particular tense in English

Perfect Future — INDICATIVE

I will have spoken

Haber (Future) + Past Participle

	Composite	PP
Yo	habré	
Tú	habrás	
Él/Ella/Usted	habrá	
Nosotros/as	habremos	
Vosotros/as	habréis	
Éllos/Ellas/Ustedes	habrán	

Example sentence in particular tense in Spanish
Example sentence in particular tense in English

Progressive Future — INDICATIVE

I am going to be speaking

Ir + a + Estar (Infinitive) + Gerund

	Composite	Gerund
Yo	voy a estar	
Tú	vas a estar	
Él/Ella/Usted	va a estar	
Nosotros/as	vamos a estar	
Vosotros/as	vais a estar	
Éllos/Ellas/Ustedes	van a estar	

Example sentence in particular tense in Spanish
Example sentence in particular tense in English

Conditional

Conditional — CONDITIONAL

I would speak

Infinitive + Endings

	Simple	Verbo
Yo	---	
Tú		
Él/Ella/Usted		
Nosotros/as		
Vosotros/as		
Éllos/Ellas/Ustedes		

Example sentence in particular tense in Spanish
Example sentence in particular tense in English

Perfect Conditional — CONDITIONAL

I would have spoken

Haber (Conditional) + Past Participle

	Compueste	PP
Yo	habría	
Tú	habrías	
Él/Ella/Usted	habría	
Nosotros/as	habríamos	
Vosotros/as	habríais	
Éllos/Ellas/Ustedes	habrían	

Example sentence in particular tense in Spanish
Example sentence in particular tense in English

Simple
Imperfect
Beginner Spanish

Perfect
Progressive
Intermediate Spanish

Verb English translation

Advanced Spanish

Past

Perfect

Progressive Perfect Preterite *INDICATIVE*

I had been speaking

Not used frequently enough to be listed here

Present

Progressive Perfect Present *INDICATIVE*

I have been speaking

Not used frequently enough to be listed here

Subjunctive

Imperfect *SUBJUNCTIVE*

...that I spoke

Stem + Endings

	Simple	Verb
...que yo	---	
...que tú		
...que Él/Ella/Usted		
...que Nosotros/as		
...que Vosotros/as		
...que Éllos/Ellas/Ustedes		

Alternative Spain conjugations

Present *SUBJUNCTIVE*

...that I speak

Stem + Endings

	Simple	Verb
...que yo	---	
...que tú		
...que Él/Ella/Usted		
...que Nosotros/as		
...que Vosotros/as		
...que Éllos/Ellas/Ustedes		

Perfect Subjunctive

Pluperfect *SUBJUNCTIVE*

...that/if I had spoken

Haber (Preterite Subjunctive) + Past Participle

	Composite	PP
...que yo	hubiera	
...que tú	hubieras	
...que Él/Ella/Usted	hubiera	
...que Nosotros/as	hubiéramos	
...que Vosotros/as	hubierais	
...que Éllos/Ellas/Ustedes	hubieran	

Alternative Spain conjugations

Perfect Present *SUBJUNCTIVE*

...that I have spoken

Haber (Present Subjunctive) + Past Participle

	Composite	PP
...que yo	haya	
...que tú	hayas	
...que Él/Ella/Usted	haya	
...que Nosotros/as	hayamos	
...que Vosotros/as	hayáis	
...que Éllos/Ellas/Ustedes	hayan	

Imperative

Commands! *IMPERATIVE*

Speak! / Don't Speak!

Stem + Endings

Tú affirmative	
Tú negative	
Usted affirmative	
Usted negative	
Vosotros/as affirmative	
Vosotros/as negative	
Ustedes affirmative	
Ustedes negative	

Applicable for 2nd person only (Single / Plural and Formal / Informal). Can be considered rude. Better to use "Necesitar" or "Poder", Tener que, or even Near Future.

 joekazemi777@gmail.com

Future

Progressive Perfect Future — INDICATIVE

I would have been speaking

Not used frequently enough to be listed here

Future — SUBJUNCTIVE

...that I will speak

Infinitive + Endings

	Simple	Verb
...que yo	---	
...que tú		
...que Él/Ella/Usted		
...que Nosotros/as		
...que Vosotros/as		
...que Éllos/Ellas/Ustedes		

Perfect Future — SUBJUNCTIVE

...that I will have spoken

Haber (Future Subjunctive) + Past Participle

	Composite	PP
...que yo	hubiere	
...que tú	hubieres	
...que Él/Ella/Usted	hubiere	
...que Nosotros/as	hubiéremos	
...que Vosotros/as	hubiereis	
...que Éllos/Ellas/Ustedes	hubieren	

Conditional

Perfect

Subjunctive

Perfect Subjunctive

Imperative

Advanced Spanish

Verbos AR regulares (hablar)

Español Principiante

Pasado — Presente

Simple

Pretérito		INDICATIVO
	I spoke	
	Stem + Endings	
	Simple	Verbos AR
Yo	---	hablé
Tú		hablaste
Él/Ella/Usted		habló
Nosotros/as		hablamos
Vosotros/as		hablisteis
Éllos/Ellas/Ustedes		hablaron

Maya habló español con Josephine.
Maya spoke Spanish with Josephine.

Presente		INDICATIVO
	I speak / I am speaking	
	Stem + Endings	
	Simple	Verbos AR
Yo	---	hablo
Tú		hablas
Él/Ella/Usted		habla
Nosotros/as		hablamos
Vosotros/as		habláis
Éllos/Ellas/Ustedes		hablan

Maya habla español con Josephine.
Maya speaks Spanish with Josephine.

Imperfecto

Imperfecto		INDICATIVO
	I used to speak	
	Stem + Endings	
	Simple	Verbos AR
Yo	---	hablaba
Tú		hablabas
Él/Ella/Usted		hablaba
Nosotros/as		hablábamos
Vosotros/as		hablabais
Éllos/Ellas/Ustedes		hablaban

Maya hablaba español con Josephine.
Maya used to speak Spanish with Josephine.

Español Intermedio

Perfecto

Pluscuamperfecto		INDICATIVO
	I had spoken	
	Haber (Past Perfect) + Past Participle	
	Compueste	PP
Yo	había	hablado
Tú	habías	
Él/Ella/Usted	había	
Nosotros/as	habíamos	
Vosotros/as	habíais	
Éllos/Ellas/Ustedes	habían	

Maya había hablado español con Josephine.
Maya had spoken Spanish with Josephine.

Presente Perfecto		INDICATIVO
	I have spoken	
	Haber (Present) + Past Participle	
	Compueste	PP
Yo	he	hablado
Tú	has	
Él/Ella/Usted	ha	
Nosotros/as	hemos	
Vosotros/as	habéis	
Éllos/Ellas/Ustedes	han	

Maya ha hablado español con Josephine.
Maya has spoken Spanish with Josephine.

Progresivo

Imperfecto Progresivo		INDICATIVO
	I was speaking	
	Estar (Imperfect) + Gerund	
	Compueste	Gerundio
Yo	estaba	hablando
Tú	estabas	
Él/Ella/Usted	estaba	
Nosotros/as	estábamos	
Vosotros/as	estabais	
Éllos/Ellas/Ustedes	estaban	

Maya estaba hablando español con Josephine.
Maya was speaking Spanish with Josephine.

Presente Progresivo		INDICATIVO
	I am speaking	
	Estar (Present) + Gerund	
	Compueste	Gerundio
Yo	estoy	hablando
Tú	estás	
Él/Ella/Usted	está	
Nosotros/as	estamos	
Vosotros/as	estáis	
Éllos/Ellas/Ustedes	están	

Maya está hablando español con Josephine.
Maya is speaking Spanish with Josephine.

 joekazemi777@gmail.com

Futuro

Futuro		INDICATIVO
I will speak		
Infinitive + Endings		
	Simple	Verbos AR
Yo	---	hablaré
Tú		hablarás
Él/Ella/Usted		hablará
Nosotros/as		hablaremos
Vosotros/as		hablaréis
Éllos/Ellas/Ustedes		hablarán
Maya hablará español con Josephine.		
Maya will speak Spanish with Josephine.		

Futuro Próximo		INDICATIVO
I am going to speak		
Ir (Present) + a + Infinitive		
	Compueste	Infinitivo
Yo	voy a	hablar
Tú	vas a	
Él/Ella/Usted	va a	
Nosotros/as	vamos a	
Vosotros/as	vais a	
Éllos/Ellas/Ustedes	van a	
Maya va a hablar español con Josephine.		
Maya is going to speak Spanish with Josephine.		

Futuro Perfecto		INDICATIVO
I will have spoken		
Haber (Future) + Past Participle		
	Compueste	PP
Yo	habré	hablado
Tú	habrás	
Él/Ella/Usted	habrá	
Nosotros/as	habremos	
Vosotros/as	habréis	
Éllos/Ellas/Ustedes	habrán	
Maya habrá hablado español con Josephine.		
Maya will have spoken Spanish with Josephine.		

Futuro Progresivo		INDICATIVO
I am going to be speaking		
Ir + a + Estar (Infinitive) + Gerund		
	Compueste	Gerundio
Yo	voy a estar	hablando
Tú	vas a estar	
Él/Ella/Usted	va a estar	
Nosotros/as	vamos a estar	
Vosotros/as	vais a estar	
Éllos/Ellas/Ustedes	van a estar	
Maya va a estar hablando español con Josephine.		
Maya is going to be speaking Spanish with Josephine		

Condicional

Condicional		CONDICIONAL
I would speak		
Infinitive + Endings		
	Simple	Verbos AR
Yo	---	hablaría
Tú		hablarías
Él/Ella/Usted		hablaría
Nosotros/as		hablaríamos
Vosotros/as		hablaríais
Éllos/Ellas/Ustedes		hablarían
Maya hablaría español con Josephine.		
Maya would speak Spanish with Josephine.		

Condicional Perfecto		CONDICIONAL
I would have spoken		
Haber (Conditional) + Past Participle		
	Compueste	PP
Yo	habría	hablado
Tú	habrías	
Él/Ella/Usted	habría	
Nosotros/as	habríamos	
Vosotros/as	habríais	
Éllos/Ellas/Ustedes	habrían	
Maya habría hablado español con Josephine.		
Maya would have spoken Spanish with Josephine.		

Simple / Imperfecto — Español Principiante

Perfecto / Progresivo — Español Intermedio

Verbos AR regulares (hablar)

Español Avanzado

Progresivo

Pasado

Pretérito Perfecto Progresivo *INDICATIVO*

I had been speaking

No se utiliza con frecuencia suficiente como para ser enumeradas aquí

Presente

Presente Perfecto Progresivo *INDICATIVO*

I have been speaking

No se utiliza con frecuencia suficiente como para ser enumeradas aquí

Subjunctivo

Imperfecto *SUBJUNCTIVO*

...that I spoke

Stem + Endings

	Simple	Verbos AR
...que yo	---	hablara
...que tú		hablaras
...que Él/Ella/Usted		hablara
...que Nosotros/as		habláramos
...que Vosotros/as		hablarais
...que Éllos/Ellas/Ustedes		hablaran

España: hablase, hablases, hablase, hablásemos, hablaseis, and hablasen

Presente Subjunctivo *SUBJUNCTIVO*

...that I speak

Stem + Endings

	Simple	Verbos AR
...que yo	---	hable
...que tú		hables
...que Él/Ella/Usted		hable
...que Nosotros/as		hablemos
...que Vosotros/as		habléis
...que Éllos/Ellas/Ustedes		hablen

Subjunctivo Perfecto

Pluscuamperfecto *SUBJUNCTIVO*

...that/if I had spoken

Haber (Preterite Subjunctive) + Past Participle

	Compueste	PP
...que yo	hubiera	hablado
...que tú	hubieras	
...que Él/Ella/Usted	hubiera	
...que Nosotros/as	hubiéramos	
...que Vosotros/as	hubierais	
...que Éllos/Ellas/Ustedes	hubieran	

España: hubiese, hubieses, hubiese, hubiésemos, hubieseis, and hubiesen

Presente Perfecto *SUBJUNCTIVO*

...that I have spoken

Haber (Present Subjunctive) + Past Participle

	Compueste	PP
...que yo	haya	hablado
...que tú	hayas	
...que Él/Ella/Usted	haya	
...que Nosotros/as	hayamos	
...que Vosotros/as	hayáis	
...que Éllos/Ellas/Ustedes	hayan	

Imperativo

¡Comandos! *IMPERATIVO*

Speak! / Don't Speak!

Stem + Endings

¡Habla tú! ¡No hables tú!	Applicable for 2nd person only (Single / Plural and Formal / Informal). Can be considered rude. Better to use "Necesitar" or "Poder", Tener que, or even Near Future.
¡Hable usted! ¡No hable usted!	
¡Hablad vosotros/as! ¡No habléis vosotros/as!	
¡Hablen ustedes! ¡No hablen ustedes!	

 joekazemi777@gmail.com

Futuro

Futuro Perfecto Progressivo *INDICATIVO*

I would have been speaking

No se utiliza con frecuencia suficiente como para ser enumeradas aquí

Futuro Subjunctivo *SUBJUNCTIVO*

...that I will speak

Infinitive + Endings

	Simple	Verbos AR
...que yo	---	hablare
...que tú		hablares
...que Él/Ella/Usted		hablare
...que Nosotros/as		habláremos
...que Vosotros/as		hablareis
...que Éllos/Ellas/Ustedes		hablaren

Futuro Perfecto *SUBJUNCTIVO*

...that I will have spoken

Haber (Future Subjunctive) + Past Participle

	Compueste	PP
...que yo	hubiere	hablado
...que tú	hubieres	
...que Él/Ella/Usted	hubiere	
...que Nosotros/as	hubiéremos	
...que Vosotros/as	hubiereis	
...que Éllos/Ellas/Ustedes	hubieren	

Condicional

Progresivo

Subjunctivo

Subjunctivo Perfecto

Imperativo

Español Avanzado

Verbos ER regulares (comer)

Español Principiante

Pasado — Simple

Pretérito		INDICATIVO
	I ate	
	Stem + Endings	
	Simple	Verbos ER
Yo	---	comí
Tú		comeste
Él/Ella/Usted		comó
Nosotros/as		comimos
Vosotros/as		comasteis
Éllos/Ellas/Ustedes		comieron

Los niños comieron sus vegetales.
The kids ate their vegetables.

Presente — Simple

Presente		INDICATIVO
	I eat / I am eating	
	Stem + Endings	
	Simple	Verbos ER
Yo	---	como
Tú		comes
Él/Ella/Usted		come
Nosotros/as		comemos
Vosotros/as		coméis
Éllos/Ellas/Ustedes		comen

Los niños comen sus vegetales.
The kids eat their vegetables.

Pasado — Imperfecto

Imperfecto		INDICATIVO
	I used to eat	
	Stem + Endings	
	Simple	Verbos ER
Yo	---	comía
Tú		comías
Él/Ella/Usted		comía
Nosotros/as		comíamos
Vosotros/as		comíais
Éllos/Ellas/Ustedes		comían

Los niños comían sus vegetales.
The kids used to eat their vegetables.

Español Intermedio

Pasado — Perfecto

Pluscuamperfecto		INDICATIVO
	I had eaten	
	Haber (Past Perfect) + Past Participle	
	Compueste	PP
Yo	había	comido
Tú	habías	
Él/Ella/Usted	había	
Nosotros/as	habíamos	
Vosotros/as	habíais	
Éllos/Ellas/Ustedes	habían	

Los niños habían comido sus vegetales.
The kids had eaten their vegetables.

Presente — Perfecto

Presente Perfecto		INDICATIVO
	I have eaten	
	Haber (Present) + Past Participle	
	Compueste	PP
Yo	he	comido
Tú	has	
Él/Ella/Usted	ha	
Nosotros/as	hemos	
Vosotros/as	habéis	
Éllos/Ellas/Ustedes	han	

Los niños han comido sus vegetales.
The kids have eaten their vegetables.

Pasado — Progresivo

Imperfecto Progresivo		INDICATIVO
	I was eating	
	Estar (Imperfect) + Gerund	
	Compueste	Gerundio
Yo	estaba	comiendo
Tú	estabas	
Él/Ella/Usted	estaba	
Nosotros/as	estábamos	
Vosotros/as	estabais	
Éllos/Ellas/Ustedes	estaban	

Los niños estaban comiendo sus vegetales.
The kids were eating their vegetables.

Presente — Progresivo

Presente Progresivo		INDICATIVO
	I am eating	
	Estar (Present) + Gerund	
	Compueste	Gerundio
Yo	estoy	comiendo
Tú	estás	
Él/Ella/Usted	está	
Nosotros/as	estamos	
Vosotros/as	estáis	
Éllos/Ellas/Ustedes	están	

Los niños están comiendo sus vegetales.
The kids are eating their vegetables.

 joekazemi777@gmail.com

Futuro

Futuro — *INDICATIVO*

I will eat

Infinitive + Endings

	Simple	Verbos ER
Yo	---	comeré
Tú		comerás
Él/Ella/Usted		comerá
Nosotros/as		comeremos
Vosotros/as		comeréis
Éllos/Ellas/Ustedes		comerán

Los niños comerán sus vegetales.
The kids will eat their vegetables.

Futuro Próximo — *INDICATIVO*

I am going to eat

Ir (Present) + a + Infinitive

	Compueste	Infinitivo
Yo	voy a	comer
Tú	vas a	
Él/Ella/Usted	va a	
Nosotros/as	vamos a	
Vosotros/as	vais a	
Éllos/Ellas/Ustedes	van a	

Los niños van a comer sus vegetales.
The kids used to eat their vegetables.

Futuro Perfecto — *INDICATIVO*

I will have eaten

Haber (Future) + Past Participle

	Compueste	PP
Yo	habré	comido
Tú	habrás	
Él/Ella/Usted	habrá	
Nosotros/as	habremos	
Vosotros/as	habréis	
Éllos/Ellas/Ustedes	habrán	

Los niños habrán comido sus vegetales.
The kids will have eaten their vegetables.

Futuro Progresivo — *INDICATIVO*

I am going to be eating

Ir + a + Estar (Infinitive) + Gerund

	Compueste	Gerundio
Yo	voy a estar	comiendo
Tú	vas a estar	
Él/Ella/Usted	va a estar	
Nosotros/as	vamos a estar	
Vosotros/as	vais a estar	
Éllos/Ellas/Ustedes	van a estar	

Los niños van a estoy comiendo sus vegetales.
The kids are going to be eating their vegetables.

Condicional

Condicional — CONDICIONAL

I would eat

Infinitive + Endings

	Simple	Verbos ER
Yo	---	comería
Tú		comerías
Él/Ella/Usted		comería
Nosotros/as		comeríamos
Vosotros/as		comeríais
Éllos/Ellas/Ustedes		comerían

Los niños comerían sus vegetales.
The kids would eat their vegetables.

Condicional Perfecto — CONDICIONAL

I would have eaten

Haber (Conditional) + Past Participle

	Compueste	PP
Yo	habría	comido
Tú	habrías	
Él/Ella/Usted	habría	
Nosotros/as	habríamos	
Vosotros/as	habríais	
Éllos/Ellas/Ustedes	habrían	

Los niños habrían comido sus vegetales.
The kids would have eaten their vegetables.

Verbos ER regulares (comer)

Español Avanzado

Progresivo

Pasado

Pretérito Perfecto Progresivo *INDICATIVO*

I had been eating

No se utiliza con frecuencia suficiente como para ser enumeradas aquí

Presente

Presente Perfecto Progresivo *INDICATIVO*

I have been eating

No se utiliza con frecuencia suficiente como para ser enumeradas aquí

Subjunctivo

Imperfecto *SUBJUNCTIVO*

...that I ate

Stem + Endings

	Simple	Verbos ER
...que yo	---	comiera
...que tú		comieras
...que Él/Ella/Usted		comiera
...que Nosotros/as		comiéramos
...que Vosotros/as		comierais
...que Éllos/Ellas/Ustedes		comieran

España: comiese, comieses, comiese, comiésemos, comieseis, and comiesen.

Presente *SUBJUNCTIVO*

...that I eat

Stem + Endings

	Simple	Verbos ER
...que yo	---	coma
...que tú		comas
...que Él/Ella/Usted		coma
...que Nosotros/as		comamos
...que Vosotros/as		comáis
...que Éllos/Ellas/Ustedes		coman

Subjunctivo Perfecto

Pluscuamperfecto *SUBJUNCTIVO*

...that/if I had eaten

Haber (Preterite Subjunctive) + Past Participle

	Compueste	PP
...que yo	hubiera	comido
...que tú	hubieras	
...que Él/Ella/Usted	hubiera	
...que Nosotros/as	hubiéramos	
...que Vosotros/as	hubierais	
...que Éllos/Ellas/Ustedes	hubieran	

España: hubiese, hubieses, hubiese, hubiésemos, hubieseis, and hubiesen

Presente Perfecto *SUBJUNCTIVO*

...that I have eaten

Haber (Present Subjunctive) + Past Participle

	Compueste	PP
...que yo	haya	comido
...que tú	hayas	
...que Él/Ella/Usted	haya	
...que Nosotros/as	hayamos	
...que Vosotros/as	hayáis	
...que Éllos/Ellas/Ustedes	hayan	

Imperativo

¡Comandos! *IMPERATIVO*

Eat! / Don't eat!

Stem + Endings

¡Come tú! ¡No comas tú!	Applicable for 2nd person only (Single / Plural and Formal / Informal). Can be considered rude. Better to use "Necesitar" or "Poder", Tener que, or even Near Future.
¡Coma usted! ¡No coma usted!!	
¡Comed vosotros/as! ¡No comáis vosotros/as!	
¡Coman ustedes! ¡No coman ustedes!	

 joekazemi777@gmail.com

Futuro

Condicional

Futuro Perfecto Progressivo *INDICATIVO*

I would have been eating

No se utiliza con frecuencia suficiente como para ser enumeradas aquí

Futuro *SUBJUNCTIVO*

...that I will eat

Infinitive (with added i) + Endings

	Simple	Verbos ER
...que yo	---	comiere
...que tú		comieres
...que Él/Ella/Usted		comiere
...que Nosotros/as		comiéremos
...que Vosotros/as		comiereis
...que Éllos/Ellas/Ustedes		comieren

Futuro Perfecto *SUBJUNCTIVO*

...that I will have eaten

Haber (Future Subjunctive) + Past Participle

	Compueste	PP
...que yo	hubiere	comido
...que tú	hubieres	
...que Él/Ella/Usted	hubiere	
...que Nosotros/as	hubiéremos	
...que Vosotros/as	hubiereis	
...que Éllos/Ellas/Ustedes	hubieren	

Progresivo

Subjunctivo

Subjunctivo Perfecto

Imperativo

Español Avanzado

Verbos IR regulares (vivir)

Español Principiante

Pasado

Simple

Pretérito *INDICATIVO*

I lived

Stem + Endings

	Simple	Verbos IR
Yo	---	viví
Tú		viveste
Él/Ella/Usted		vivó
Nosotros/as		vivimos
Vosotros/as		vivisteis
Éllos/Ellas/Ustedes		vivieron

Nosotros vivimos cerca del parque.
We lived near the park.

Imperfecto

Imperfecto *INDICATIVO*

I used to live

Stem + Endings

	Simple	Verbos IR
Yo	---	vivía
Tú		vivías
Él/Ella/Usted		vivía
Nosotros/as		vivíamos
Vosotros/as		vivíais
Éllos/Ellas/Ustedes		vivían

Nosotros vivíamos cerca del parque.
We used to live near the park.

Presente

Presente *INDICATIVO*

I live / I am living

Stem + Endings

	Simple	Verbos IR
Yo	---	vivo
Tú		vives
Él/Ella/Usted		vive
Nosotros/as		vivimos
Vosotros/as		vivís
Éllos/Ellas/Ustedes		viven

Nosotros vivimos cerca del parque.
We live near the park.

Español Intermedio

Perfecto

Pluscuamperfecto *INDICATIVO*

I had lived

Haber (Past Perfect) + Past Participle

	Compueste	PP
Yo	había	vivido
Tú	habías	
Él/Ella/Usted	había	
Nosotros/as	habíamos	
Vosotros/as	habíais	
Éllos/Ellas/Ustedes	habían	

Nosotros habíamos vivido cerca del parque.
We had lived near the park.

Presente Perfecto *INDICATIVO*

I have lived

Haber (Present) + Past Participle

	Compueste	PP
Yo	he	vivido
Tú	has	
Él/Ella/Usted	ha	
Nosotros/as	hemos	
Vosotros/as	habéis	
Éllos/Ellas/Ustedes	han	

Nosotros hemos vivido cerca del parque.
We have lived near the park.

Progresivo

Imperfecto Progresivo *INDICATIVO*

I was living

Estar (Imperfect) + Gerund

	Compueste	Gerundio
Yo	estaba	viviendo
Tú	estabas	
Él/Ella/Usted	estaba	
Nosotros/as	estábamos	
Vosotros/as	estabais	
Éllos/Ellas/Ustedes	estaban	

Nosotros estábamos viviendo cerca del parque.
We were living near the park.

Presente Progresivo *INDICATIVO*

I am living

Estar (Present) + Gerund

	Compueste	Gerundio
Yo	estoy	viviendo
Tú	estás	
Él/Ella/Usted	está	
Nosotros/as	estamos	
Vosotros/as	estáis	
Éllos/Ellas/Ustedes	están	

Nosotros estamos viviendo cerca del parque.
We are living near the park.

 joekazemi777@gmail.com

Futuro

Futuro — INDICATIVO

I will live

Infinitive + Endings

	Simple	Verbos IR
Yo	---	viviré
Tú		vivirás
Él/Ella/Usted		vivirá
Nosotros/as		viviremos
Vosotros/as		viviréis
Éllos/Ellas/Ustedes		vivirán

Nosotros viviremos cerca del parque.
We will live near the park.

Futuro Próximo — INDICATIVO

I am going to live

Ir (Present) + a + Infinitive

	Compueste	Infinitivo
Yo	voy a	vivir
Tú	vas a	
Él/Ella/Usted	va a	
Nosotros/as	vamos a	
Vosotros/as	vais a	
Éllos/Ellas/Ustedes	van a	

Nosotros vamos a vivir cerca del parque.
We are going to live near the park.

Futuro Perfecto — INDICATIVO

I will have lived

Haber (Future) + Past Participle

	Compueste	PP
Yo	habré	vivido
Tú	habrás	
Él/Ella/Usted	habrá	
Nosotros/as	habremos	
Vosotros/as	habréis	
Éllos/Ellas/Ustedes	habrán	

Nosotros habremos vivido cerca del parque.
We will have lived near the park.

Futuro Progresivo — INDICATIVO

I am going to be living

Ir + a + Estar (Infinitive) + Gerund

	Compueste	Gerundio
Yo	voy a estar	viviendo
Tú	vas a estar	
Él/Ella/Usted	va a estar	
Nosotros/as	vamos a estar	
Vosotros/as	vais a estar	
Éllos/Ellas/Ustedes	van a estar	

Nosotros vamos a estar viviendo cerca del parque.
We are going to be living near the park.

Condicional

Condicional — CONDICIONAL

I would live

Infinitive + Endings

	Simple	Verbos IR
Yo	---	viviría
Tú		vivirías
Él/Ella/Usted		viviría
Nosotros/as		viviríamos
Vosotros/as		viviríais
Éllos/Ellas/Ustedes		vivirían

Nosotros viviríamos cerca del parque.
We would live near the park.

Condicional Perfecto — CONDICIONAL

I would have lived

Haber (Conditional) + Past Participle

	Compueste	PP
Yo	habría	vivido
Tú	habrías	
Él/Ella/Usted	habría	
Nosotros/as	habríamos	
Vosotros/as	habríais	
Éllos/Ellas/Ustedes	habrían	

Nosotros habríamos vivido cerca del parque.
We would have lived near the park.

Verbos IR regulares (vivir)

Español Avanzado

Pasado

Progresivo

Pretérito Perfecto Progresivo *INDICATIVO*

I had been living

No se utiliza con frecuencia suficiente como para ser enumeradas aquí

Subjunctivo

Imperfecto Subjunctivo *SUBJUNCTIVO*

...that I lived

Stem + Endings

	Simple	Verbos IR
...que yo	---	viviera
...que tú		vivieras
...que Él/Ella/Usted		viviera
...que Nosotros/as		viviéramos
...que Vosotros/as		vivierais
...que Éllos/Ellas/Ustedes		vivieran

España: viviese, vivieses, viviese, viviésemos, vivieseis, and viviesen.

Subjunctivo Perfecto

Pluscuamperfecto *SUBJUNCTIVO*

...that/if I had lived

Haber (Preterite Subjunctive) + Past Participle

	Compueste	PP
...que yo	hubiera	vivido
...que tú	hubieras	
...que Él/Ella/Usted	hubiera	
...que Nosotros/as	hubiéramos	
...que Vosotros/as	hubierais	
...que Éllos/Ellas/Ustedes	hubieran	

España: hubiese, hubieses, hubiese, hubiésemos, hubieseis, and hubiesen.

Imperativo

Presente

Progresivo

Presente Perfecto Progresivo *INDICATIVO*

I have been living

No se utiliza con frecuencia suficiente como para ser enumeradas aquí

Subjunctivo

Presente Subjunctivo *SUBJUNCTIVO*

...that I live

Stem + Endings

	Simple	Verbos IR
...que yo	---	viva
...que tú		viv as
...que Él/Ella/Usted		viva
...que Nosotros/as		vivamos
...que Vosotros/as		viváis
...que Éllos/Ellas/Ustedes		vivan

Subjunctivo Perfecto

Presente Perfecto *SUBJUNCTIVO*

...that I have lived

Haber (Present Subjunctive) + Past Participle

	Compueste	PP
...que yo	haya	vivido
...que tú	hayas	
...que Él/Ella/Usted	haya	
...que Nosotros/as	hayamos	
...que Vosotros/as	hayáis	
...que Éllos/Ellas/Ustedes	hayan	

Imperativo

¡Comandos! *IMPERATIVO*

Live! / Don't live!

Stem + Endings

¡Vive tú! ¡No vivas tú!	Applicable for 2nd person only (Single / Plural and Formal / Informal). Can be considered rude. Better to use "Necesitar" or "Poder", Tener que, or even Near Future.
¡Viva usted! ¡No viva usted!	
¡Vivid vosotros/as! ¡No viváis vosotros/as!	
¡Vivan ustedes! ¡No vivan ustedes!	

 joekazemi777@gmail.com

Futuro | Condicional

Futuro Perfecto Progressivo INDICATIVO

I would have been living

No se utiliza con frecuencia suficiente como para ser enumeradas aquí

Futuro Subjunctivo SUBJUNCTIVO

...that I will live

Infinitive (with added e) + Endings

	Simple	Verbos IR
...que yo	---	viviere
...que tú		vivieres
...que Él/Ella/Usted		viviere
...que Nosotros/as		viviéremos
...que Vosotros/as		viviereis
...que Éllos/Ellas/Ustedes		vivieren

Futuro Perfecto SUBJUNCTIVO

...that I will have lived

Haber (Future Subjunctive) + Past Participle

	Compueste	PP
...que yo	hubiere	vivido
...que tú	hubieres	
...que Él/Ella/Usted	hubiere	
...que Nosotros/as	hubiéremos	
...que Vosotros/as	hubiereis	
...que Éllos/Ellas/Ustedes	hubieren	

Progresivo

Subjunctivo

Subjunctivo Perfecto

Imperativo

Blank

Los verbos ***irregulares*** *más utilizados en español*

Estos son algunos de los verbos irregulares más utilizados en español. Cada uno se merece su propia tabla. Cualquier persona seria sobre el aprendizaje de las necesidades españolas de memorizar sus tiempos y conjugaciones. Sólo las tablas de principiantes e intermedios se les da para estos verbos.

These are some of the most commonly used irregular verbs in Spanish. Each deserves it's own table. Anyone serious about learning Spanish needs to memorize their tenses and conjugations. Only the beginner and intermediate tables are given for these verbs.

I ***haber***	*to have (* ***impersonal*** *)*
II ***haber***	*to have (* ***auxiliary*** *)*
1 ***ser***	*to be (permanent)*
2 ***estar***	*to be (temporary)*
3 ***tener***	*to have*
4 ***ir***	*to go*
5 ***poder***	*to be able*
6 ***poner***	*to put*
7 ***querer***	*to want*
8 ***saber***	*to know*
9 ***decir***	*to say*
10 ***venir***	*to come*
11 ***ver***	*to see*
12 ***dar***	*to give*
13 ***salir***	*to leave*
14 ***pensar***	*to think / to plan*
15 ***traer***	*to bring / to carry*
16 ***abrir***	*to open*
17 ***jugar***	*to play*

Notice that while we had one big table for each type of regular verbs (i.e. AR, ER, and IR regual verb types) we now need a separate table for each irregular verb.

I

haber — to have (impersonal)

Pasado / Presente

Español Principiante

Simple

Pretérito — INDICATIVO

There was... / There were...

Hubo...

Hubo una oportunidad.
There was an opportunity.

Presente — INDICATIVO

There is... / There are...

Hay...

Hay una oportunidad.
There is an opportunity.

Imperfecto

Imperfecto — INDICATIVO

There used to be...

Había...

Había una oportunidad.
There used to be an opportunity.

Español Intermedio

Perfecto

Pluscuamperfecto — INDICATIVO

There had been...

Había habido...

Había habido una oportunidad.
There had been an opportunity.

Presente Perfecto — INDICATIVO

There has been... / There have been...

Ha habido...

Ha habido una oportunidad.
There has been an opportunity.

Progresivo

 joekazemi777@gmail.com

Futuro

Futuro INDICATIVO

There will be...

Habrá...

Habrá una oportunidad.
There will be an opportunity.

Condicional

Condicional CONDICIONAL

There would be...

Habría...

Habría una oportunidad.
There would be an opportunity.

Futuro Perfecto INDICATIVO

There will have been...

Habrá habido...

Habrá habido una oportunidad.
There will have been an opportunity.

Condicional Perfecto CONDICIONAL

There would have been...

Habría habido...

Habría habido una oportunidad.
There would have been an opportunity.

Simple Imperfecto

Español Principiante

Perfecto Progresivo

Español Intermedio

II

haber — to have (auxiliary)

Pasado | Presente

Español Principiante — Simple

Pretérito — *INDICATIVO*

I had

Irregular

	Simple	Verbo
Yo	---	hube
Tú		hubiste
Él/Ella/Usted		hubo
Nosotros/as		hubimos
Vosotros/as		hubisteis
Éllos/Ellas/Ustedes		hubieron

Presente — *INDICATIVO*

I have / I am having

Irregular

	Simple	Verbo
Yo	---	he
Tú		has
Él/Ella/Usted		ha
Nosotros/as		hemos
Vosotros/as		habéis
Éllos/Ellas/Ustedes		han

Imperfecto

Imperfecto — *INDICATIVO*

I used to have

Irregular

	Simple	Verbo
Yo	---	había
Tú		habías
Él/Ella/Usted		había
Nosotros/as		habíamos
Vosotros/as		habíais
Éllos/Ellas/Ustedes		habían

Español Intermedio — Perfecto

Pluscuamperfecto — *INDICATIVO*

I had had

Haber (Past Perfect) + Past Participle

	Compueste	PP
Yo	había	habido
Tú	habías	
Él/Ella/Usted	había	
Nosotros/as	habíamos	
Vosotros/as	habíais	
Éllos/Ellas/Ustedes	habían	

Presente Perfecto — *INDICATIVO*

I have had

Haber (Present) + Past Participle

	Compueste	PP
Yo	he	habido
Tú	has	
Él/Ella/Usted	ha	
Nosotros/as	hemos	
Vosotros/as	habéis	
Éllos/Ellas/Ustedes	han	

Progresivo

Imperfecto Progresivo — *INDICATIVO*

I was having

Estar (Imperfect) + Gerund

	Compueste	Gerundio
Yo	estaba	habiendo
Tú	estabas	
Él/Ella/Usted	estaba	
Nosotros/as	estábamos	
Vosotros/as	estabais	
Éllos/Ellas/Ustedes	estaban	

Presente Progresivo — *INDICATIVO*

I am having

Estar (Present) + Gerund

	Compueste	Gerundio
Yo	estoy	habiendo
Tú	estás	
Él/Ella/Usted	está	
Nosotros/as	estamos	
Vosotros/as	estáis	
Éllos/Ellas/Ustedes	están	

 joekazemi777@gmail.com

Futuro

Condicional

Futuro		*INDICATIVO*
	I will have	
	Irregular	
	Simple	Verbo
Yo	---	habré
Tú		habrás
Él/Ella/Usted		habrá
Nosotros/as		habremos
Vosotros/as		habréis
Éllos/Ellas/Ustedes		habrán

Condicional		CONDICIONAL
	I would have	
	Irregular	
	Simple	Verbo
Yo	---	habría
Tú		habrías
Él/Ella/Usted		habría
Nosotros/as		habríamos
Vosotros/as		habríais
Éllos/Ellas/Ustedes		habrían

Futuro Próximo		*INDICATIVO*
	I am going to have	
	Ir (Present) + a + Infinitive	
	Compueste	Infinitivo
Yo	voy a	haber
Tú	vas a	
Él/Ella/Usted	va a	
Nosotros/as	vamos a	
Vosotros/as	vais a	
Éllos/Ellas/Ustedes	van a	

Futuro Perfecto		*INDICATIVO*
	I will have had	
	Haber (Future) + Past Participle	
	Compueste	PP
Yo	habré	habido
Tú	habrás	
Él/Ella/Usted	habrá	
Nosotros/as	habremos	
Vosotros/as	habréis	
Éllos/Ellas/Ustedes	habrán	

Condicional Perfecto		CONDICIONAL
	I would have had	
	Haber (Conditional) + Past Participle	
	Compueste	PP
Yo	habría	habido
Tú	habrías	
Él/Ella/Usted	habría	
Nosotros/as	habríamos	
Vosotros/as	habríais	
Éllos/Ellas/Ustedes	habrían	

Futuro Progresivo		*INDICATIVO*
	I am going to be having	
	Ir + a + Estar (Infinitive) + Gerund	
	Compueste	Gerundio
Yo	voy a estar	habiendo
Tú	vas a estar	
Él/Ella/Usted	va a estar	
Nosotros/as	vamos a estar	
Vosotros/as	vais a estar	
Éllos/Ellas/Ustedes	van a estar	

Simple *Imperfecto* Español Principiante

Perfecto *Progresivo* Español Intermedio

1

ser — to be (permanent)

Español Principiante

Pasado / Presente

Simple

Pretérito		INDICATIVO
	I was	
	Irregular	
	Simple	Verbo
Yo	---	fui
Tú		fuiste
Él/Ella/Usted		fue
Nosotros/as		fuimos
Vosotros/as		fuisteis
Éllos/Ellas/Ustedes		fueron

La abuela de Maya fue generosa.
Maya's grandmother was generous.

Presente		INDICATIVO
	I am / I am being	
	Irregular	
	Simple	Verbo
Yo	---	soy
Tú		eres
Él/Ella/Usted		es
Nosotros/as		somos
Vosotros/as		sois
Éllos/Ellas/Ustedes		son

La abuela de Maya es generosa.
Maya's grandmother is generous.

Imperfecto

Imperfecto		INDICATIVO
	I used to be	
	Irregular	
	Simple	Verbo
Yo	---	era
Tú		eras
Él/Ella/Usted		era
Nosotros/as		éramos
Vosotros/as		erais
Éllos/Ellas/Ustedes		eran

La abuela de Maya era generosa.
Maya's grandmother used to be generous.

Español Intermedio

Perfecto

Pluscuamperfecto		INDICATIVO
	I had been	
	Haber (Past Perfect) + Past Participle	
	Compueste	PP
Yo	había	sido
Tú	habías	
Él/Ella/Usted	había	
Nosotros/as	habíamos	
Vosotros/as	habíais	
Éllos/Ellas/Ustedes	habían	

La abuela de Maya había sido generosa.
Maya's grandmother had been generous.

Presente Perfecto		INDICATIVO
	I have been	
	Haber (Present) + Past Participle	
	Compueste	PP
Yo	he	sido
Tú	has	
Él/Ella/Usted	ha	
Nosotros/as	hemos	
Vosotros/as	habéis	
Éllos/Ellas/Ustedes	han	

La abuela de Maya ha sido generosa.
Maya's grandmother has been generous.

Progresivo

Imperfecto Progresivo		INDICATIVO
	I was being	
	Estar (Imperfect) + Gerund	
	Compueste	Gerundio
Yo	estaba	siendo
Tú	estabas	
Él/Ella/Usted	estaba	
Nosotros/as	estábamos	
Vosotros/as	estabais	
Éllos/Ellas/Ustedes	estaban	

La abuela de Maya estaba siendo generosa.
Maya's grandmother was being generous.

Presente Progresivo		INDICATIVO
	I am being	
	Estar (Present) + Gerund	
	Compueste	Gerundio
Yo	estoy	siendo
Tú	estás	
Él/Ella/Usted	está	
Nosotros/as	estamos	
Vosotros/as	estáis	
Éllos/Ellas/Ustedes	están	

La abuela de Maya está siendo generosa.
Maya's grandmother is being generous.

 joekazemi777@gmail.com

Futuro

Futuro		INDICATIVO
	I will be	
	Irregular	
	Simple	Verbo
Yo	---	seré
Tú		serás
Él/Ella/Usted		será
Nosotros/as		seremos
Vosotros/as		seréis
Éllos/Ellas/Ustedes		serán
La abuela de Maya <u>será</u> generosa.		
Maya's grandmother <u>will be</u> generous.		

Futuro Próximo		INDICATIVO
	I am going to speak	
	Ir (Present) + a + Infinitive	
	Compueste	Infinitivo
Yo	voy a	ser
Tú	vas a	
Él/Ella/Usted	va a	
Nosotros/as	vamos a	
Vosotros/as	vais a	
Éllos/Ellas/Ustedes	van a	
Maya's grandmother <u>va a ser</u> generous.		
Maya's grandmother <u>va a ser</u> generous.		

Futuro Perfecto		INDICATIVO
	I will have been	
	Haber (Future) + Past Participle	
	Compueste	PP
Yo	habré	sido
Tú	habrás	
Él/Ella/Usted	habrá	
Nosotros/as	habremos	
Vosotros/as	habréis	
Éllos/Ellas/Ustedes	habrán	
La abuela de Maya <u>habrá sido</u> generosa.		
Maya's grandmother <u>will have been</u> generous.		

Futuro Progresivo		INDICATIVO
	I am going to be being	
	Ir + a + Estar (Infinitive) + Gerund	
	Compueste	Gerundio
Yo	voy a estar	siendo
Tú	vas a estar	
Él/Ella/Usted	va a estar	
Nosotros/as	vamos a estar	
Vosotros/as	vais a estar	
Éllos/Ellas/Ustedes	van a estar	
La abuela de Maya <u>va a estar siendo</u> generosa.		
Maya's grandmother <u>is going to be being</u> generous.		

Condicional

Condicional		CONDICIONAL
	I would be	
	Irregular	
	Simple	Verbo
Yo	---	sería
Tú		serías
Él/Ella/Usted		sería
Nosotros/as		seríamos
Vosotros/as		seríais
Éllos/Ellas/Ustedes		serían
La abuela de Maya <u>sería</u> generosa.		
Maya's grandmother <u>would be</u> generous.		

Condicional Perfecto		CONDICIONAL
	I would have been	
	Haber (Conditional) + Past Participle	
	Compueste	PP
Yo	habría	sido
Tú	habrías	
Él/Ella/Usted	habría	
Nosotros/as	habríamos	
Vosotros/as	habríais	
Éllos/Ellas/Ustedes	habrían	
La abuela de Maya <u>habría sido</u> generosa.		
Maya's grandmother <u>would have been</u> generous.		

Simple

Imperfecto

Español Principiante

Perfecto

Progresivo

Español Intermedio

2

estar — to be (temporary)

Español Principiante

Pasado

Simple

Pretérito		INDICATIVO
	I was	
	Irregular	
	Simple	Verbo
Yo	---	estuve
Tú		estuviste
Él/Ella/Usted		estuvo
Nosotros/as		estuvimos
Vosotros/as		estuvisteis
Éllos/Ellas/Ustedes		estuvieron

Maya estuvo muy feliz.
Maya was very happy.

Imperfecto

Imperfecto		INDICATIVO
	I used to be	
	Irregular	
	Simple	Verbo
Yo	---	estaba
Tú		estabas
Él/Ella/Usted		estaba
Nosotros/as		estábamos
Vosotros/as		estabais
Éllos/Ellas/Ustedes		estabais

Maya estaba muy feliz.
Maya used to be very happy.

Presente

Presente		INDICATIVO
	I am / I am being	
	Irregular	
	Simple	Verbo
Yo	---	estoy
Tú		estás
Él/Ella/Usted		está
Nosotros/as		estamos
Vosotros/as		estáis
Éllos/Ellas/Ustedes		están

Maya está muy feliz.
Maya is very happy.

Español Intermedio

Perfecto

Pluscuamperfecto		INDICATIVO
	I had been	
	Haber (Past Perfect) + Past Participle	
	Compueste	PP
Yo	había	estado
Tú	habías	
Él/Ella/Usted	había	
Nosotros/as	habíamos	
Vosotros/as	habíais	
Éllos/Ellas/Ustedes	habían	

Maya había estado muy feliz.
Maya had been very happy.

Presente Perfecto		INDICATIVO
	I have been	
	Haber (Present) + Past Participle	
	Compueste	PP
Yo	he	estado
Tú	has	
Él/Ella/Usted	ha	
Nosotros/as	hemos	
Vosotros/as	habéis	
Éllos/Ellas/Ustedes	han	

Maya ha estado muy feliz.
Maya has been very happy.

Progresivo

Imperfecto Progresivo		INDICATIVO
	I was being	
	Estar (Imperfect) + Gerund	
	Compueste	Gerundio
Yo	estaba	estando
Tú	estabas	
Él/Ella/Usted	estaba	
Nosotros/as	estábamos	
Vosotros/as	estabais	
Éllos/Ellas/Ustedes	estaban	

Maya estaba estando muy feliz.
Maya was being very happy.

Presente Progresivo		INDICATIVO
	I am being	
	Estar (Present) + Gerund	
	Compueste	Gerundio
Yo	estoy	estando
Tú	estás	
Él/Ella/Usted	está	
Nosotros/as	estamos	
Vosotros/as	estáis	
Éllos/Ellas/Ustedes	están	

Maya está estando muy feliz.
Maya is being very happy.

 joekazemi777@gmail.com

Futuro

Futuro — INDICATIVO

I will be

Irregular

	Simple	Verbo
Yo	---	estaré
Tú		estarás
Él/Ella/Usted		estará
Nosotros/as		estaremos
Vosotros/as		estaréis
Éllos/Ellas/Ustedes		estarán

Maya <u>estará</u> muy feliz.
Maya <u>will be</u> very happy.

Futuro Próximo — INDICATIVO

I am going to speak

Ir (Present) + a + Infinitive

	Compueste	Infinitivo
Yo	voy a	estar
Tú	vas a	
Él/Ella/Usted	va a	
Nosotros/as	vamos a	
Vosotros/as	vais a	
Éllos/Ellas/Ustedes	van a	

Maya <u>va a estar</u> muy feliz.
Maya <u>is going to be</u> very happy.

Futuro Perfecto — INDICATIVO

I will have been

Haber (Future) + Past Participle

	Compueste	PP
Yo	habré	estado
Tú	habrás	
Él/Ella/Usted	habrá	
Nosotros/as	habremos	
Vosotros/as	habréis	
Éllos/Ellas/Ustedes	habrán	

Maya <u>habrá estado</u> muy feliz.
Maya <u>will have been</u> very happy.

Futuro Progresivo — INDICATIVO

I am going to be being

Ir + a + Estar (Infinitive) + Gerund

	Compueste	Gerundio
Yo	voy a estar	estando
Tú	vas a estar	
Él/Ella/Usted	va a estar	
Nosotros/as	vamos a estar	
Vosotros/as	vais a estar	
Éllos/Ellas/Ustedes	van a estar	

Maya <u>va a estar estando</u> muy feliz.
Maya <u>is going to be being</u> very happy.

Condicional

Condicional — CONDICIONAL

I would be

Irregular

	Simple	Verbo
Yo	---	estaría
Tú		estarías
Él/Ella/Usted		estaría
Nosotros/as		estaríamos
Vosotros/as		estaríais
Éllos/Ellas/Ustedes		estarían

Maya <u>estaría</u> muy feliz.
Maya <u>would be</u> very happy.

Condicional Perfecto — CONDICIONAL

I would have been

Haber (Conditional) + Past Participle

	Compueste	PP
Yo	habría	estado
Tú	habrías	
Él/Ella/Usted	habría	
Nosotros/as	habríamos	
Vosotros/as	habríais	
Éllos/Ellas/Ustedes	habrían	

Maya <u>habría estado</u> muy feliz.
Maya <u>would have been</u> very happy.

3

tener — to have

Pasado / Presente

Español Principiante — Simple

Pretérito		INDICATIVO
	I had	
	Irregular	
	Simple	Verbo
Yo	---	tuve
Tú		tuviste
Él/Ella/Usted		tuvo
Nosotros/as		tuvimos
Vosotros/as		tuvisteis
Éllos/Ellas/Ustedes		tuvieron
Nosotros tuvimos un perro.		
We had a dog.		

Presente		INDICATIVO
	I have / I am having	
	Irregular	
	Simple	Verbo
Yo	---	tengo
Tú		tienes
Él/Ella/Usted		tiene
Nosotros/as		tenemos
Vosotros/as		tenéis
Éllos/Ellas/Ustedes		tienen
Nosotros tenemos un perro.		
We have a dog.		

Imperfecto

Imperfecto		INDICATIVO
	I used to have	
	Irregular	
	Simple	Verbo
Yo	---	tenía
Tú		tenías
Él/Ella/Usted		tenía
Nosotros/as		teníamos
Vosotros/as		teníais
Éllos/Ellas/Ustedes		tenían
Nosotros teníamos un perro.		
We used to have a dog.		

Español Intermedio — Perfecto

Pluscuamperfecto		INDICATIVO
	I had had	
	Haber (Past Perfect) + Past Participle	
	Compueste	PP
Yo	había	tenido
Tú	habías	
Él/Ella/Usted	había	
Nosotros/as	habíamos	
Vosotros/as	habíais	
Éllos/Ellas/Ustedes	habían	
Nosotros habíamos tenido un perro.		
We had had a dog.		

Presente Perfecto		INDICATIVO
	I have had	
	Haber (Present) + Past Participle	
	Compueste	PP
Yo	he	tenido
Tú	has	
Él/Ella/Usted	ha	
Nosotros/as	hemos	
Vosotros/as	habéis	
Éllos/Ellas/Ustedes	han	
Nosotros hemos tenido un perro.		
We have had a dog.		

Español Progresivo

Imperfecto Progresivo		INDICATIVO
	I was having	
	Estar (Imperfect) + Gerund	
	Compueste	Gerundio
Yo	estaba	teniendo
Tú	estabas	
Él/Ella/Usted	estaba	
Nosotros/as	estábamos	
Vosotros/as	estabais	
Éllos/Ellas/Ustedes	estaban	
Nosotros habíamos teniendo un perro.		
We were having a dog.		

Presente Progresivo		INDICATIVO
	I am having	
	Estar (Present) + Gerund	
	Compueste	Gerundio
Yo	estoy	teniendo
Tú	estás	
Él/Ella/Usted	está	
Nosotros/as	estamos	
Vosotros/as	estáis	
Éllos/Ellas/Ustedes	están	
Nosotros estamos teniendo un perro.		
We are having a dog.		

 joekazemi777@gmail.com

Futuro

Futuro *INDICATIVO*

I will have

Irregular

	Simple	Verbo
Yo	---	tendré
Tú		tendrás
Él/Ella/Usted		tendrá
Nosotros/as		tendremos
Vosotros/as		tendréis
Éllos/Ellas/Ustedes		tendrán

Nosotros tendremos un perro.
We will have a dog.

Futuro Próximo *INDICATIVO*

I am going to have

Ir (Present) + a + Infinitive

	Compueste	Infinitivo
Yo	voy a	tener
Tú	vas a	
Él/Ella/Usted	va a	
Nosotros/as	vamos a	
Vosotros/as	vais a	
Éllos/Ellas/Ustedes	van a	

Nosotros vamos a tener un perro.
We are going to have a dog.

Futuro Perfecto *INDICATIVO*

I will have had

Haber (Future) + Past Participle

	Compueste	PP
Yo	habré	tenido
Tú	habrás	
Él/Ella/Usted	habrá	
Nosotros/as	habremos	
Vosotros/as	habréis	
Éllos/Ellas/Ustedes	habrán	

Nosotros habremos tenido un perro.
We will have had a dog.

Futuro Progresivo *INDICATIVO*

I am going to be having

Ir + a + Estar (Infinitive) + Gerund

	Compueste	Gerundio
Yo	voy a estar	teniendo
Tú	vas a estar	
Él/Ella/Usted	va a estar	
Nosotros/as	vamos a estar	
Vosotros/as	vais a estar	
Éllos/Ellas/Ustedes	van a estar	

Nosotros estamos teniendo un perro.
We are having a dog.

Condicional

Condicional CONDICIONAL

I would have

Irregular

	Simple	Verbo
Yo	---	tendría
Tú		tendrías
Él/Ella/Usted		tendría
Nosotros/as		tendríamos
Vosotros/as		tendríais
Éllos/Ellas/Ustedes		tendrían

Nosotros tendríamos un perro.
We would have a dog.

Condicional Perfecto CONDICIONAL

I would have had

Haber (Conditional) + Past Participle

	Compueste	PP
Yo	habría	tenido
Tú	habrías	
Él/Ella/Usted	habría	
Nosotros/as	habríamos	
Vosotros/as	habríais	
Éllos/Ellas/Ustedes	habrían	

Nosotros habríamos tenido un perro.
We would have had a dog.

Simple *Imperfecto* Español Principiante

Perfecto *Progresivo* Español Intermedio

4

ir *to go*

Español Principiante

Pasado

Simple

Pretérito		*INDICATIVO*
	I went	
	Irregular	
	Simple	Verbo
Yo	---	fui
Tú		fuiste
Él/Ella/Usted		fue
Nosotros/as		fuimos
Vosotros/as		fuisteis
Éllos/Ellas/Ustedes		fueron

Nosotros fuimos a México por vacaciones.
We went to Mexico for vacation.

Imperfecto

Imperfecto		*INDICATIVO*
	I used to go	
	Irregular	
	Simple	Verbo
Yo	---	iba
Tú		ibas
Él/Ella/Usted		iba
Nosotros/as		íbamos
Vosotros/as		ibais
Éllos/Ellas/Ustedes		iban

Nosotros íbamos a México por vacaciones.
We used to go to Mexico for vacation.

Presente

Presente		*INDICATIVO*
	I go / I am going	
	Irregular	
	Simple	Verbo
Yo	---	voy
Tú		vas
Él/Ella/Usted		va
Nosotros/as		vamos
Vosotros/as		vais
Éllos/Ellas/Ustedes		van

Nosotros vamos a México por vacaciones.
We go to Mexico for vacation.

Español Intermedio

Perfecto

Pluscuamperfecto		*INDICATIVO*
	I had gone	
	Haber (Past Perfect) + Past Participle	
	Compueste	PP
Yo	había	ido
Tú	habías	
Él/Ella/Usted	había	
Nosotros/as	habíamos	
Vosotros/as	habíais	
Éllos/Ellas/Ustedes	habían	

Nosotros habíamos ido a México por vacaciones.
We had gone to Mexico for vacation.

Presente Perfecto		*INDICATIVO*
	I have gone	
	Haber (Present) + Past Participle	
	Compueste	PP
Yo	he	ido
Tú	has	
Él/Ella/Usted	ha	
Nosotros/as	hemos	
Vosotros/as	habéis	
Éllos/Ellas/Ustedes	han	

Nosotros hemos ido a México por vacaciones.
We have gone to Mexico for vacation.

Progresivo

Imperfecto Progresivo		*INDICATIVO*
	I was going	
	Estar (Imperfect) + Gerund	
	Compueste	Gerundio
Yo	estaba	yendo
Tú	estabas	
Él/Ella/Usted	estaba	
Nosotros/as	estábamos	
Vosotros/as	estabais	
Éllos/Ellas/Ustedes	estaban	

Nosotros estábamos yendo a México por vacaciones.
We were going to Mexico for vacation.

Presente Progresivo		*INDICATIVO*
	I am going	
	Estar (Present) + Gerund	
	Compueste	Gerundio
Yo	estoy	yendo
Tú	estás	
Él/Ella/Usted	está	
Nosotros/as	estamos	
Vosotros/as	estáis	
Éllos/Ellas/Ustedes	están	

Nosotros estamos yendo a México por vacaciones.
We are going to Mexico for vacation.

 joekazemi777@gmail.com

Futuro

Futuro		*INDICATIVO*
	I will go	
	Irregular	
	Simple	Verbo
Yo	---	iré
Tú		irás
Él/Ella/Usted		irá
Nosotros/as		iremos
Vosotros/as		iréis
Éllos/Ellas/Ustedes		irán

Nosotros iremos a México por vacaciones.
We will go to Mexico for vacation.

Futuro Próximo		*INDICATIVO*
	I am going to go	
	Ir (Present) + a + Infinitive	
	Compueste	Infinitivo
Yo	voy a	ir
Tú	vas a	
Él/Ella/Usted	va a	
Nosotros/as	vamos a	
Vosotros/as	vais a	
Éllos/Ellas/Ustedes	van a	

Nosotros vamos a ir a México por vacaciones.
We are going to go to Mexico for vacation.

Futuro Perfecto		*INDICATIVO*
	I will have gone	
	Haber (Future) + Past Participle	
	Compueste	PP
Yo	habré	ido
Tú	habrás	
Él/Ella/Usted	habrá	
Nosotros/as	habremos	
Vosotros/as	habréis	
Éllos/Ellas/Ustedes	habrán	

Nosotros habremos ido a México por vacaciones.
We will have gone to Mexico for vacation.

Futuro Progresivo		*INDICATIVO*
	I am going to be going	
	Ir + a + Estar (Infinitive) + Gerund	
	Compueste	Gerundio
Yo	voy a estar	yendo
Tú	vas a estar	
Él/Ella/Usted	va a estar	
Nosotros/as	vamos a estar	
Vosotros/as	vais a estar	
Éllos/Ellas/Ustedes	van a estar	

Nosotros vamos a estar yendo a México por vacacior
We are going to be going to Mexico for vacation.

Condicional

Condicional		CONDICIONAL
	I would go	
	Irregular	
	Simple	Verbo
Yo	---	iría
Tú		irías
Él/Ella/Usted		iría
Nosotros/as		iríamos
Vosotros/as		iríais
Éllos/Ellas/Ustedes		irían

Nosotros iremos a México por vacaciones.
We will go to Mexico for vacation.

Condicional Perfecto		CONDICIONAL
	I would have gone	
	Haber (Conditional) + Past Participle	
	Compueste	PP
Yo	habría	ido
Tú	habrías	
Él/Ella/Usted	habría	
Nosotros/as	habríamos	
Vosotros/as	habríais	
Éllos/Ellas/Ustedes	habrían	

Nosotros habríamos ido a México por vacaciones.
We would have gone to Mexico for vacation.

Simple *Imperfecto* Español Principiante

Perfecto *Progresivo* Español Intermedio

5

poder — to be able

Español Principiante

Pasado

Simple

Pretérito		INDICATIVO
	I was able	
	Irregular	
	Simple	Verbo
Yo	---	pude
Tú		pudiste
Él/Ella/Usted		pudo
Nosotros/as		pudimos
Vosotros/as		pudisteis
Éllos/Ellas/Ustedes		pudieron
Ellas pudieron nadar.		
They were able to swim.		

Imperfecto

Imperfecto		INDICATIVO
	I used to be able	
	Irregular	
	Simple	Verbo
Yo	---	podía
Tú		podías
Él/Ella/Usted		podía
Nosotros/as		podíamos
Vosotros/as		podíais
Éllos/Ellas/Ustedes		podían
Ellas podían nadar.		
They used to be able to swim.		

Presente

Presente		INDICATIVO
	I am able / I am being able	
	Irregular	
	Simple	Verbo
Yo	---	puedo
Tú		puedes
Él/Ella/Usted		puede
Nosotros/as		podemos
Vosotros/as		podéis
Éllos/Ellas/Ustedes		pueden
Ellas pueden nadar.		
They are able to swim.		

Español Intermedio

Perfecto

Pluscuamperfecto		INDICATIVO
	I had been able	
	Haber (Past Perfect) + Past Participle	
	Compueste	PP
Yo	había	podido
Tú	habías	
Él/Ella/Usted	había	
Nosotros/as	habíamos	
Vosotros/as	habíais	
Éllos/Ellas/Ustedes	habían	
Ellas habían podido nadar.		
They had been able to swim.		

Presente Perfecto		INDICATIVO
	I have been able	
	Haber (Present) + Past Participle	
	Compueste	PP
Yo	he	podido
Tú	has	
Él/Ella/Usted	ha	
Nosotros/as	hemos	
Vosotros/as	habéis	
Éllos/Ellas/Ustedes	han	
Ellas han podido nadar.		
They have been able to swim.		

Progresivo

Imperfecto Progresivo		INDICATIVO
	I was being able	
	Estar (Imperfect) + Gerund	
	Compueste	Gerundio
Yo	estaba	podiendo
Tú	estabas	
Él/Ella/Usted	estaba	
Nosotros/as	estábamos	
Vosotros/as	estabais	
Éllos/Ellas/Ustedes	estaban	
Ellas estaban podiendo nadar.		
They were being able to swim.		

Presente Progresivo		INDICATIVO
	I am being able	
	Estar (Present) + Gerund	
	Compueste	Gerundio
Yo	estoy	podiendo
Tú	estás	
Él/Ella/Usted	está	
Nosotros/as	estamos	
Vosotros/as	estáis	
Éllos/Ellas/Ustedes	están	
Ellas están podiendo nadar.		
They are being able to swim.		

 joekazemi777@gmail.com

Futuro

Futuro *INDICATIVO*

I will be able

Irregular

	Simple	Verbo
Yo	---	podré
Tú		podrás
Él/Ella/Usted		podrá
Nosotros/as		podremos
Vosotros/as		podréis
Éllos/Ellas/Ustedes		podrán

Ellas podrán nadar.
They will be able to swim.

Futuro Próximo *INDICATIVO*

I am going to be able

Ir (Present) + a + Infinitive

	Compueste	Infinitivo
Yo	voy a	poder
Tú	vas a	
Él/Ella/Usted	va a	
Nosotros/as	vamos a	
Vosotros/as	vais a	
Éllos/Ellas/Ustedes	van a	

Ellas van a poder nadar.
They are going to be able to to swim.

Futuro Perfecto *INDICATIVO*

I will have been able

Haber (Future) + Past Participle

	Compueste	PP
Yo	habré	podido
Tú	habrás	
Él/Ella/Usted	habrá	
Nosotros/as	habremos	
Vosotros/as	habréis	
Éllos/Ellas/Ustedes	habrán	

Ellas habrán podido nadar.
They will have been able to swim.

Futuro Progresivo *INDICATIVO*

I am going to be being able

Ir + a + Estar (Infinitive) + Gerund

	Compueste	Gerundio
Yo	voy a estar	podiendo
Tú	vas a estar	
Él/Ella/Usted	va a estar	
Nosotros/as	vamos a estar	
Vosotros/as	vais a estar	
Éllos/Ellas/Ustedes	van a estar	

Ellas están podiendo nadar.
They are being able to swim.

Condicional

Condicional *CONDICIONAL*

I would be able

Irregular

	Simple	Verbo
Yo	---	podría
Tú		podrías
Él/Ella/Usted		podría
Nosotros/as		podríamos
Vosotros/as		podríais
Éllos/Ellas/Ustedes		podrían

Ellas podrían nadar.
They would be able to swim.

Condicional Perfecto *CONDICIONAL*

I would have been able

Haber (Conditional) + Past Participle

	Compueste	PP
Yo	habría	podido
Tú	habrías	
Él/Ella/Usted	habría	
Nosotros/as	habríamos	
Vosotros/as	habríais	
Éllos/Ellas/Ustedes	habrían	

Ellas habrían podido nadar.
They would have been able to swim.

Simple
Imperfecto
Español Principiante

Perfecto
Progresivo
Español Intermedio

6 poner — to put

Español Principiante

Pasado

Simple

Pretérito		*INDICATIVO*
	I put	
	Irregular	
	Simple	Verbo
Yo	---	puse
Tú		pusiste
Él/Ella/Usted		puso
Nosotros/as		pusimos
Vosotros/as		pusisteis
Éllos/Ellas/Ustedes		pusieron

Yo puse los libros sobre la mesa.
I put the books on the table.

Imperfecto

Imperfecto		*INDICATIVO*
	I used to put	
	Irregular	
	Simple	Verbo
Yo	---	ponía
Tú		ponías
Él/Ella/Usted		ponía
Nosotros/as		poníamos
Vosotros/as		poníais
Éllos/Ellas/Ustedes		ponían

Yo ponía los libros sobre la mesa.
I used to put the books on the table.

Presente

Presente		*INDICATIVO*
	I put / I am putting	
	Irregular	
	Simple	Verbo
Yo	---	pongo
Tú		pones
Él/Ella/Usted		pones
Nosotros/as		ponemos
Vosotros/as		ponéis
Éllos/Ellas/Ustedes		ponen

Yo pongo los libros sobre la mesa.
I put the books on the table.

Español Intermedio

Perfecto

Pluscuamperfecto		*INDICATIVO*
	I had put	
	Haber (Past Perfect) + Past Participle	
	Compueste	PP
Yo	había	puesto
Tú	habías	
Él/Ella/Usted	había	
Nosotros/as	habíamos	
Vosotros/as	habíais	
Éllos/Ellas/Ustedes	habían	

Yo había puesto los libros sobre la mesa.
I had put the books on the table.

Presente Perfecto		*INDICATIVO*
	I have put	
	Haber (Present) + Past Participle	
	Compueste	PP
Yo	he	puesto
Tú	has	
Él/Ella/Usted	ha	
Nosotros/as	hemos	
Vosotros/as	habéis	
Éllos/Ellas/Ustedes	han	

Yo he puesto los libros sobre la mesa.
I have put the books on the table.

Progresivo

Imperfecto Progresivo		*INDICATIVO*
	I was putting	
	Estar (Imperfect) + Gerund	
	Compueste	Gerundio
Yo	estaba	poniendo
Tú	estabas	
Él/Ella/Usted	estaba	
Nosotros/as	estábamos	
Vosotros/as	estabais	
Éllos/Ellas/Ustedes	estaban	

Yo estaba poniendo los libros sobre la mesa.
I was putting the books on the table.

Presente Progresivo		*INDICATIVO*
	I am putting	
	Estar (Present) + Gerund	
	Compueste	Gerundio
Yo	estoy	poniendo
Tú	estás	
Él/Ella/Usted	está	
Nosotros/as	estamos	
Vosotros/as	estáis	
Éllos/Ellas/Ustedes	están	

Yo estoy poniendo los libros sobre la mesa.
I am putting the books on the table.

Futuro

Futuro		*INDICATIVO*
	I will put	
	Irregular	
	Simple	Verbo
Yo	---	pondré
Tú		pondrás
Él/Ella/Usted		pondrá
Nosotros/as		pondremos
Vosotros/as		pondréis
Éllos/Ellas/Ustedes		pondrán

Yo pondré los libros sobre la mesa.
I will put the books on the table.

Futuro Próximo		*INDICATIVO*
	I am going to put	
	Ir (Present) + a + Infinitive	
	Compueste	Infinitivo
Yo	voy a	poner
Tú	vas a	
Él/Ella/Usted	va a	
Nosotros/as	vamos a	
Vosotros/as	vais a	
Éllos/Ellas/Ustedes	van a	

Yo voy a poner los libros sobre la mesa.
I am going to put the books on the table.

Futuro Perfecto		*INDICATIVO*
	I will have put	
	Haber (Future) + Past Participle	
	Compueste	PP
Yo	habré	puesto
Tú	habrás	
Él/Ella/Usted	habrá	
Nosotros/as	habremos	
Vosotros/as	habréis	
Éllos/Ellas/Ustedes	habrán	

Yo habré puesto los libros sobre la mesa.
I will have put the books on the table.

Futuro Progresivo		*INDICATIVO*
	I am going to be putting	
	Ir + a + Estar (Infinitive) + Gerund	
	Compueste	Gerundio
Yo	voy a estar	poniendo
Tú	vas a estar	
Él/Ella/Usted	va a estar	
Nosotros/as	vamos a estar	
Vosotros/as	vais a estar	
Éllos/Ellas/Ustedes	van a estar	

Yo voy a estar poniendo los libros sobre la mesa.
I am going to be putting the books on the table.

Condicional

Condicional		*CONDICIONAL*
	I would put	
	Irregular	
	Simple	Verbo
Yo	---	pondría
Tú		pondrías
Él/Ella/Usted		pondría
Nosotros/as		pondríamos
Vosotros/as		pondríais
Éllos/Ellas/Ustedes		pondrían

Yo pondría los libros sobre la mesa.
I would put the books on the table.

Condicional Perfecto		*CONDICIONAL*
	I would have put	
	Haber (Conditional) + Past Participle	
	Compueste	PP
Yo	habría	puesto
Tú	habrías	
Él/Ella/Usted	habría	
Nosotros/as	habríamos	
Vosotros/as	habríais	
Éllos/Ellas/Ustedes	habrían	

Yo habría puesto los libros sobre la mesa.
I would have put the books on the table.

Simple
Imperfecto
Español Principiante

Perfecto
Progresivo
Español Intermedio

7

querer — to want

Español Principiante

Pasado

Simple

Pretérito — *INDICATIVO*

I wanted

Irregular

	Simple	Verbo
Yo	---	quise
Tú		quisiste
Él/Ella/Usted		quiso
Nosotros/as		quisimos
Vosotros/as		quisisteis
Éllos/Ellas/Ustedes		quisieron

Éllos quisieron justicia.
They wanted justice.

Imperfecto

Imperfecto — *INDICATIVO*

I used to want

Irregular

	Simple	Verbo
Yo	---	quería
Tú		querías
Él/Ella/Usted		quería
Nosotros/as		queríamos
Vosotros/as		queríais
Éllos/Ellas/Ustedes		querían

Éllos querían justicia.
They used to want justice.

Presente

Presente — *INDICATIVO*

I want / I am wanting

Irregular

	Simple	Verbo
Yo	---	quiero
Tú		quieres
Él/Ella/Usted		quiere
Nosotros/as		queremos
Vosotros/as		queréis
Éllos/Ellas/Ustedes		quieren

Éllos quieren justicia.
They want justice.

Español Intermedio

Perfecto

Pluscuamperfecto — *INDICATIVO*

I had wanted

Haber (Past Perfect) + Past Participle

	Compueste	PP
Yo	había	querido
Tú	habías	
Él/Ella/Usted	había	
Nosotros/as	habíamos	
Vosotros/as	habíais	
Éllos/Ellas/Ustedes	habían	

Éllos habían querido justicia.
They had wanted justice.

Presente Perfecto — *INDICATIVO*

I have wanted

Haber (Present) + Past Participle

	Compueste	PP
Yo	he	querido
Tú	has	
Él/Ella/Usted	ha	
Nosotros/as	hemos	
Vosotros/as	habéis	
Éllos/Ellas/Ustedes	han	

Éllos han querido justicia.
They have wanted justice.

Progresivo

Imperfecto Progresivo — *INDICATIVO*

I was wanting

Estar (Imperfect) + Gerund

	Compueste	Gerundio
Yo	estaba	queriendo
Tú	estabas	
Él/Ella/Usted	estaba	
Nosotros/as	estábamos	
Vosotros/as	estabais	
Éllos/Ellas/Ustedes	estaban	

Éllos estaban queriendo justicia.
They were wanting justice.

Presente Progresivo — *INDICATIVO*

I am wanting

Estar (Present) + Gerund

	Compueste	Gerundio
Yo	estoy	queriendo
Tú	estás	
Él/Ella/Usted	está	
Nosotros/as	estamos	
Vosotros/as	estáis	
Éllos/Ellas/Ustedes	están	

Éllos están queriendo justicia.
They are wanting justice.

 joekazemi777@gmail.com

Futuro

Futuro		*INDICATIVO*
	I will want	
	Irregular	
	Simple	Verbo
Yo	---	querré
Tú		querrás
Él/Ella/Usted		querrá
Nosotros/as		querremos
Vosotros/as		querréis
Éllos/Ellas/Ustedes		querrán

Éllos querrán justicia.
They will want justice.

Futuro Próximo		*INDICATIVO*
	I am going to want	
	Ir (Present) + a + Infinitive	
	Compueste	Infinitivo
Yo	voy a	querer
Tú	vas a	
Él/Ella/Usted	va a	
Nosotros/as	vamos a	
Vosotros/as	vais a	
Éllos/Ellas/Ustedes	van a	

Éllos van a querer justicia.
They are going to want justice.

Futuro Perfecto		*INDICATIVO*
	I will have wanted	
	Haber (Future) + Past Participle	
	Compueste	PP
Yo	habré	querido
Tú	habrás	
Él/Ella/Usted	habrá	
Nosotros/as	habremos	
Vosotros/as	habréis	
Éllos/Ellas/Ustedes	habrán	

Éllos habrán querido justicia.
They will have wanted justice.

Futuro Progresivo		*INDICATIVO*
	I am going to be wanting	
	Ir + a + Estar (Infinitive) + Gerund	
	Compueste	Gerundio
Yo	voy a estar	queriendo
Tú	vas a estar	
Él/Ella/Usted	va a estar	
Nosotros/as	vamos a estar	
Vosotros/as	vais a estar	
Éllos/Ellas/Ustedes	van a estar	

Éllos van a estar queriendo justicia.
They are going to be wanting justice.

Condicional

Condicional		*CONDICIONAL*
	I would want	
	Irregular	
	Simple	Verbo
Yo	---	querría
Tú		querrías
Él/Ella/Usted		querría
Nosotros/as		querríamos
Vosotros/as		querríais
Éllos/Ellas/Ustedes		querrían

Éllos querrían justicia.
They would want justice.

Condicional Perfecto		*CONDICIONAL*
	I would have wanted	
	Haber (Conditional) + Past Participle	
	Compueste	PP
Yo	habría	querido
Tú	habrías	
Él/Ella/Usted	habría	
Nosotros/as	habríamos	
Vosotros/as	habríais	
Éllos/Ellas/Ustedes	habrían	

Éllos habrían querido justicia.
They would have wanted justice.

Simple *Imperfecto* — *Español Principiante*

Perfecto *Progresivo* — *Español Intermedio*

8

saber — to know

Español Principiante

Pasado — Simple

Pretérito		INDICATIVO
	I knew	
	Irregular	
	Simple	Verbo
Yo	---	supe
Tú		supiste
Él/Ella/Usted		supo
Nosotros/as		supimos
Vosotros/as		supisteis
Éllos/Ellas/Ustedes		supieron

Tú supiste la historia del arte muy bien.
You knew art history very well.

Presente — Simple

Presente		INDICATIVO
	I know / I am knowing	
	Irregular	
	Simple	Verbo
Yo	---	sé
Tú		sabes
Él/Ella/Usted		sabe
Nosotros/as		sabemos
Vosotros/as		sabéis
Éllos/Ellas/Ustedes		saben

Tú sabes la historia del arte muy bien.
You know art history very well.

Pasado — Imperfecto

Imperfecto		INDICATIVO
	I used to know	
	Irregular	
	Simple	Verbo
Yo	---	sabía
Tú		sabías
Él/Ella/Usted		sabía
Nosotros/as		sabíamos
Vosotros/as		sabíais
Éllos/Ellas/Ustedes		sabían

Tú sabías la historia del arte muy bien.
You used to know art history very well.

Español Intermedio

Pasado — Perfecto

Pluscuamperfecto		INDICATIVO
	I had known	
	Haber (Past Perfect) + Past Participle	
	Compueste	PP
Yo	había	sabido
Tú	habías	
Él/Ella/Usted	había	
Nosotros/as	habíamos	
Vosotros/as	habíais	
Éllos/Ellas/Ustedes	habían	

Tú habías sabido la historia del arte muy bien.
You had known art history very well.

Presente — Perfecto

Presente Perfecto		INDICATIVO
	I have known	
	Haber (Present) + Past Participle	
	Compueste	PP
Yo	he	sabido
Tú	has	
Él/Ella/Usted	ha	
Nosotros/as	hemos	
Vosotros/as	habéis	
Éllos/Ellas/Ustedes	han	

Tú has sabido la historia del arte muy bien.
You have known art history very well.

Pasado — Progresivo

Imperfecto Progresivo		INDICATIVO
	I was knowing	
	Estar (Imperfect) + Gerund	
	Compueste	Gerundio
Yo	estaba	sabiendo
Tú	estabas	
Él/Ella/Usted	estaba	
Nosotros/as	estábamos	
Vosotros/as	estabais	
Éllos/Ellas/Ustedes	estaban	

Tú estabas sabiendo la historia del arte muy bien.
You were knowing art history very well.

Presente — Progresivo

Presente Progresivo		INDICATIVO
	I am knowing	
	Estar (Present) + Gerund	
	Compueste	Gerundio
Yo	estoy	sabiendo
Tú	estás	
Él/Ella/Usted	está	
Nosotros/as	estamos	
Vosotros/as	estáis	
Éllos/Ellas/Ustedes	están	

Tú estás sabiendo la historia del arte muy bien.
You were knowing art history very well.

 joekazemi777@gmail.com

Futuro

Condicional

Futuro *INDICATIVO*

I will know

Irregular

	Simple	Verbo
Yo	---	sabré
Tú		sabrás
Él/Ella/Usted		sabrá
Nosotros/as		sabremos
Vosotros/as		sabréis
Éllos/Ellas/Ustedes		sabrán

Tú sabrás la historia del arte muy bien.
You will know art history very well.

Condicional CONDICIONAL

I would know

Irregular

	Simple	Verbo
Yo	---	sabría
Tú		sabrías
Él/Ella/Usted		sabría
Nosotros/as		sabríamos
Vosotros/as		sabríais
Éllos/Ellas/Ustedes		sabrían

Tú sabrías la historia del arte muy bien.
You would know art history very well.

Futuro Próximo *INDICATIVO*

I am going to know

Ir (Present) + a + Infinitive

	Compueste	Infinitivo
Yo	voy a	saber
Tú	vas a	
Él/Ella/Usted	va a	
Nosotros/as	vamos a	
Vosotros/as	vais a	
Éllos/Ellas/Ustedes	van a	

Tú vas a saber la historia del arte muy bien.
You are going to know art history very well.

Simple Imperfecto — Español Principiante

Futuro Perfecto *INDICATIVO*

I will have known

Haber (Future) + Past Participle

	Compueste	PP
Yo	habré	sabido
Tú	habrás	
Él/Ella/Usted	habrá	
Nosotros/as	habremos	
Vosotros/as	habréis	
Éllos/Ellas/Ustedes	habrán	

Tú habrás sabido la historia del arte muy bien.
You will have known art history very well.

Condicional Perfecto CONDICIONAL

I would have known

Haber (Conditional) + Past Participle

	Compueste	PP
Yo	habría	sabido
Tú	habrías	
Él/Ella/Usted	habría	
Nosotros/as	habríamos	
Vosotros/as	habríais	
Éllos/Ellas/Ustedes	habrían	

Tú habrías sabido la historia del arte muy bien.
You would have known art history very well.

Futuro Progresivo *INDICATIVO*

I am going to be knowing

Ir + a + Estar (Infinitive) + Gerund

	Compueste	Gerundio
Yo	voy a estar	sabiendo
Tú	vas a estar	
Él/Ella/Usted	va a estar	
Nosotros/as	vamos a estar	
Vosotros/as	vais a estar	
Éllos/Ellas/Ustedes	van a estar	

Tú vas a estar sabiendo la historia del arte muy bien.
You are going to be knowing art history very well.

Perfecto Progresivo — Español Intermedio

9

decir — to say

Español Principiante

Pasado — Simple

Pretérito		INDICATIVO
	I said	
	Irregular	
	Simple	Verbo
Yo	---	dije
Tú		dijiste
Él/Ella/Usted		dijo
Nosotros/as		dijimos
Vosotros/as		dijisteis
Éllos/Ellas/Ustedes		dijeron

Maya dijo hola a todos.
Maya said hello to everyone.

Presente — Simple

Presente		INDICATIVO
	I say / I am saying	
	Irregular	
	Simple	Verbo
Yo	---	digo
Tú		dices
Él/Ella/Usted		dice
Nosotros/as		decimos
Vosotros/as		decís
Éllos/Ellas/Ustedes		dicen

Maya dice hola a todos.
Maya says hello to everyone.

Pasado — Imperfecto

Imperfecto		INDICATIVO
	I used to say	
	Irregular	
	Simple	Verbo
Yo	---	decía
Tú		decías
Él/Ella/Usted		decía
Nosotros/as		decíamos
Vosotros/as		decíais
Éllos/Ellas/Ustedes		decían

Maya decía hola a todos.
Maya used to say hello to everyone.

Español Intermedio

Perfecto

Pluscuamperfecto		INDICATIVO
	I had said	
	Haber (Past Perfect) + Past Participle	
	Compueste	PP
Yo	había	dicho
Tú	habías	
Él/Ella/Usted	había	
Nosotros/as	habíamos	
Vosotros/as	habíais	
Éllos/Ellas/Ustedes	habían	

Maya había dicho hola a todos.
Maya had said hello to everyone.

Presente Perfecto		INDICATIVO
	I have said	
	Haber (Present) + Past Participle	
	Compueste	PP
Yo	he	dicho
Tú	has	
Él/Ella/Usted	ha	
Nosotros/as	hemos	
Vosotros/as	habéis	
Éllos/Ellas/Ustedes	han	

Maya ha dicho hola a todos.
Maya has said hello to everyone.

Progresivo

Imperfecto Progresivo		INDICATIVO
	I was saying	
	Estar (Imperfect) + Gerund	
	Compueste	Gerundio
Yo	estaba	diciendo
Tú	estabas	
Él/Ella/Usted	estaba	
Nosotros/as	estábamos	
Vosotros/as	estabais	
Éllos/Ellas/Ustedes	estaban	

Maya estaba diciendo hola a todos.
Maya was saying hello to everyone.

Presente Progresivo		INDICATIVO
	I am saying	
	Estar (Present) + Gerund	
	Compueste	Gerundio
Yo	estoy	diciendo
Tú	estás	
Él/Ella/Usted	está	
Nosotros/as	estamos	
Vosotros/as	estáis	
Éllos/Ellas/Ustedes	están	

Maya está diciendo hola a todos.
Maya is saying hello to everyone.

 joekazemi777@gmail.com

Futuro

Futuro		INDICATIVO
	I will say	
	Irregular	
	Simple	Verbo
Yo	---	diré
Tú		dirás
Él/Ella/Usted		dirá
Nosotros/as		diremos
Vosotros/as		diréis
Éllos/Ellas/Ustedes		dirán
Maya dirá hola a todos.		
Maya will say hello to everyone.		

Futuro Próximo		INDICATIVO
	I am going to say	
	Ir (Present) + a + Infinitive	
	Compueste	Infinitivo
Yo	voy a	decir
Tú	vas a	
Él/Ella/Usted	va a	
Nosotros/as	vamos a	
Vosotros/as	vais a	
Éllos/Ellas/Ustedes	van a	
Maya va a decir hola a todos.		
Maya is going to say hello to everyone.		

Futuro Perfecto		INDICATIVO
	I will have said	
	Haber (Future) + Past Participle	
	Compueste	PP
Yo	habré	dicho
Tú	habrás	
Él/Ella/Usted	habrá	
Nosotros/as	habremos	
Vosotros/as	habréis	
Éllos/Ellas/Ustedes	habrán	
Maya habrá dicho hola a todos.		
Maya will have said hello to everyone.		

Futuro Progresivo		INDICATIVO
	I am going to be saying	
	Ir + a + Estar (Infinitive) + Gerund	
	Compueste	Gerundio
Yo	voy a estar	diciendo
Tú	vas a estar	
Él/Ella/Usted	va a estar	
Nosotros/as	vamos a estar	
Vosotros/as	vais a estar	
Éllos/Ellas/Ustedes	van a estar	
Maya va a estar diciendo hola a todos.		
Maya is going to be saying hello to everyone.		

Condicional

Condicional		CONDICIONAL
	I would say	
	Irregular	
	Simple	Verbo
Yo	---	diría
Tú		dirías
Él/Ella/Usted		diría
Nosotros/as		diríamos
Vosotros/as		diríais
Éllos/Ellas/Ustedes		dirían
Maya diría hola a todos.		
Maya would say hello to everyone.		

Condicional Perfecto		CONDICIONAL
	I would have said	
	Haber (Conditional) + Past Participle	
	Compueste	PP
Yo	habría	dicho
Tú	habrías	
Él/Ella/Usted	habría	
Nosotros/as	habríamos	
Vosotros/as	habríais	
Éllos/Ellas/Ustedes	habrían	
Maya habría dicho hola a todos.		
Maya would have said hello to everyone.		

Simple Imperfecto Español Principiante

Perfecto Progresivo Español Intermedio

10

venir — to come

Español Principiante

Pasado

Simple

Pretérito	I came (Irregular)	INDICATIVO
	Simple	Verbo
Yo	---	verní
Tú		verniste
Él/Ella/Usted		vernió
Nosotros/as		vernimos
Vosotros/as		vernisteis
Éllos/Ellas/Ustedes		vernieron

Mamá vernió a casa en metro.
Mom came home by subway.

Imperfecto

Imperfecto Pasado	I used to come (Irregular)	INDICATIVO
	Simple	Verbo
Yo	---	vernía
Tú		vernías
Él/Ella/Usted		vernía
Nosotros/as		verníamos
Vosotros/as		verníais
Éllos/Ellas/Ustedes		vernían

Mamá vernía a casa en metro.
Mom used to come home by subway.

Presente

Presente	I come / I am coming (Irregular)	INDICATIVO
	Simple	Verbo
Yo	---	verno
Tú		vernes
Él/Ella/Usted		verne
Nosotros/as		vernimos
Vosotros/as		vernís
Éllos/Ellas/Ustedes		vernen

Mamá viene a casa en metro.
Mom comes home by subway.

Español Intermedio

Perfecto

Pluscuamperfecto	I had come — Haber (Past Perfect) + Past Participle	INDICATIVO
	Compueste	PP
Yo	había	vernido
Tú	habías	
Él/Ella/Usted	había	
Nosotros/as	habíamos	
Vosotros/as	habíais	
Éllos/Ellas/Ustedes	habían	

Mamá había vernido a casa en metro.
Mom had come home by subway.

Presente Perfecto	I have come — Haber (Present) + Past Participle	INDICATIVO
	Compueste	PP
Yo	he	vernido
Tú	has	
Él/Ella/Usted	ha	
Nosotros/as	hemos	
Vosotros/as	habéis	
Éllos/Ellas/Ustedes	han	

Mamá ha vernido a casa en metro.
Mom has come home by subway.

Progresivo

Imperfecto Progresivo	I was coming — Estar (Imperfect) + Gerund	INDICATIVO
	Compueste	Gerundio
Yo	estaba	verniendo
Tú	estabas	
Él/Ella/Usted	estaba	
Nosotros/as	estábamos	
Vosotros/as	estabais	
Éllos/Ellas/Ustedes	estaban	

Mamá estaba verniendo a casa en metro.
Mom was coming home by subway.

Presente Progresivo	I am coming — Estar (Present) + Gerund	INDICATIVO
	Compueste	Gerundio
Yo	estoy	verniendo
Tú	estás	
Él/Ella/Usted	está	
Nosotros/as	estamos	
Vosotros/as	estáis	
Éllos/Ellas/Ustedes	están	

Mamá está verniendo a casa en metro.
Mom is coming home by subway.

 joekazemi777@gmail.com

Futuro

Futuro — INDICATIVO

I will come

Irregular

	Simple	Verbo
Yo	---	verniré
Tú		vernirás
Él/Ella/Usted		vernirá
Nosotros/as		verniremos
Vosotros/as		verniréis
Éllos/Ellas/Ustedes		vernirán

Mamá vernirá a casa en metro.
Mom will come home by subway.

Futuro Próximo — INDICATIVO

I am going to come

Ir (Present) + a + Infinitive

	Compueste	Infinitivo
Yo	voy a	vernir
Tú	vas a	
Él/Ella/Usted	va a	
Nosotros/as	vamos a	
Vosotros/as	vais a	
Éllos/Ellas/Ustedes	van a	

Mamá va a venir a casa en metro.
Mom is going to come home by subway.

Futuro Perfecto — INDICATIVO

I will have come

Haber (Future) + Past Participle

	Compueste	PP
Yo	habré	vernido
Tú	habrás	
Él/Ella/Usted	habrá	
Nosotros/as	habremos	
Vosotros/as	habréis	
Éllos/Ellas/Ustedes	habrán	

Mamá habrá vernido a casa en metro.
Mom will have come home by subway.

Futuro Progresivo — INDICATIVO

I am going to be coming

Ir + a + Estar (Infinitive) + Gerund

	Compueste	Gerundio
Yo	voy a estar	verniendo
Tú	vas a estar	
Él/Ella/Usted	va a estar	
Nosotros/as	vamos a estar	
Vosotros/as	vais a estar	
Éllos/Ellas/Ustedes	van a estar	

Mamá va a estar verniendo a casa en metro.
Mom is going to be coming home by subway.

Condicional

Condicional — CONDICIONAL

I would come

Irregular

	Simple	Verbo
Yo	---	verniría
Tú		vernirías
Él/Ella/Usted		verniría
Nosotros/as		verniríamos
Vosotros/as		verniríais
Éllos/Ellas/Ustedes		vernirían

Mamá verniría a casa en metro.
Mom would come home by subway.

Condicional Perfecto — CONDICIONAL

I would have come

Haber (Conditional) + Past Participle

	Compueste	PP
Yo	habría	vernido
Tú	habrías	
Él/Ella/Usted	habría	
Nosotros/as	habríamos	
Vosotros/as	habríais	
Éllos/Ellas/Ustedes	habrían	

Mamá habría vernido a casa en metro.
Mom would have come home by subway.

Simple *Imperfecto* — Español Principiante

Perfecto *Progresivo* — Español Intermedio

11

ver — to see

Español Principiante

Pasado

Simple

Pretérito		*INDICATIVO*
	I saw	
	Irregular	
	Simple	Verbo
Yo	---	vi
Tú		viste
Él/Ella/Usted		vio
Nosotros/as		vimos
Vosotros/as		visteis
Éllos/Ellas/Ustedes		vieron

Yo vi la salida del sol.
I saw the sunrise.

Imperfecto

Imperfecto		*INDICATIVO*
	I used to see	
	Irregular	
	Simple	Verbo
Yo	---	veía
Tú		veías
Él/Ella/Usted		veía
Nosotros/as		veíamos
Vosotros/as		veíais
Éllos/Ellas/Ustedes		veían

Yo veía la salida del sol.
I used to see the sunrise.

Presente

Presente		*INDICATIVO*
	I see / I am seeing	
	Irregular	
	Simple	Verbo
Yo	---	veo
Tú		ves
Él/Ella/Usted		ve
Nosotros/as		vemos
Vosotros/as		veis
Éllos/Ellas/Ustedes		ven

Yo veo la salida del sol.
I see the sunrise.

Español Intermedio

Perfecto

Pluscuamperfecto		*INDICATIVO*
	I had seen	
	Haber (Past Perfect) + Past Participle	
	Compueste	PP
Yo	había	visto
Tú	habías	
Él/Ella/Usted	había	
Nosotros/as	habíamos	
Vosotros/as	habíais	
Éllos/Ellas/Ustedes	habían	

Yo había visto la salida del sol.
I had seen the sunrise.

Presente Perfecto		*INDICATIVO*
	I have seen	
	Haber (Present) + Past Participle	
	Compueste	PP
Yo	he	visto
Tú	has	
Él/Ella/Usted	ha	
Nosotros/as	hemos	
Vosotros/as	habéis	
Éllos/Ellas/Ustedes	han	

Yo he visto la salida del sol.
I have seen the sunrise.

Progresivo

Imperfecto Progresivo		*INDICATIVO*
	I was seeing	
	Estar (Imperfect) + Gerund	
	Compueste	Gerundio
Yo	estaba	viendo
Tú	estabas	
Él/Ella/Usted	estaba	
Nosotros/as	estábamos	
Vosotros/as	estabais	
Éllos/Ellas/Ustedes	estaban	

Yo estaba viendo la salida del sol.
I was seeing the sunrise.

Presente Progresivo		*INDICATIVO*
	I am seeing	
	Estar (Present) + Gerund	
	Compueste	Gerundio
Yo	estoy	viendo
Tú	estás	
Él/Ella/Usted	está	
Nosotros/as	estamos	
Vosotros/as	estáis	
Éllos/Ellas/Ustedes	están	

Yo estoy viendo la salida del sol.
I am seeing the sunrise.

 joekazemi777@gmail.com

Futuro

Futuro *INDICATIVO*

I will see

Irregular

	Simple	Verbo
Yo	---	veré
Tú		verás
Él/Ella/Usted		verá
Nosotros/as		veremos
Vosotros/as		veréis
Éllos/Ellas/Ustedes		verán

Yo veré la salida del sol.
I will see the sunrise.

Futuro Próximo *INDICATIVO*

I am going to see

Ir (Present) + a + Infinitive

	Compueste	Infinitivo
Yo	voy a	ver
Tú	vas a	
Él/Ella/Usted	va a	
Nosotros/as	vamos a	
Vosotros/as	vais a	
Éllos/Ellas/Ustedes	van a	

Yo voy a ver la salida del sol.
I am going to see the sunrise.

Futuro Perfecto *INDICATIVO*

I will have seen

Haber (Future) + Past Participle

	Compueste	PP
Yo	habré	visto
Tú	habrás	
Él/Ella/Usted	habrá	
Nosotros/as	habremos	
Vosotros/as	habréis	
Éllos/Ellas/Ustedes	habrán	

Yo habré visto la salida del sol.
I will have seen the sunrise.

Futuro Progresivo *INDICATIVO*

I am going to be seeing

Ir + a + Estar (Infinitive) + Gerund

	Compueste	Gerundio
Yo	voy a estar	viendo
Tú	vas a estar	
Él/Ella/Usted	va a estar	
Nosotros/as	vamos a estar	
Vosotros/as	vais a estar	
Éllos/Ellas/Ustedes	van a estar	

Yo voy a estar viendo la salida del sol.
I am going to be seeing the sunrise.

Condicional

Condicional CONDICIONAL

I would see

Irregular

	Simple	Verbo
Yo	---	vería
Tú		verías
Él/Ella/Usted		vería
Nosotros/as		veríamos
Vosotros/as		veríais
Éllos/Ellas/Ustedes		verían

Yo vería la salida del sol.
I would see the sunrise.

Condicional Perfecto CONDICIONAL

I would have seen

Haber (Conditional) + Past Participle

	Compueste	PP
Yo	habría	visto
Tú	habrías	
Él/Ella/Usted	habría	
Nosotros/as	habríamos	
Vosotros/as	habríais	
Éllos/Ellas/Ustedes	habrían	

Yo habría visto la salida del sol.
I would have seen the sunrise.

Simple
Imperfecto
Español Principiante

Perfecto
Progresivo
Español Intermedio

12

dar — to give

Español Principiante

Pasado

Simple

Pretérito		INDICATIVO
	I gave	
	Irregular	
	Simple	Verbo
Yo	---	di
Tú		diste
Él/Ella/Usted		dio
Nosotros/as		dimos
Vosotros/as		disteis
Éllos/Ellas/Ustedes		dieron

Ustedes dieron buenos regalos.
You gave nice gifts.

Imperfecto

Imperfecto		INDICATIVO
	I used to give	
	Irregular	
	Simple	Verbo
Yo	---	daba
Tú		dabas
Él/Ella/Usted		daba
Nosotros/as		dábamos
Vosotros/as		dabais
Éllos/Ellas/Ustedes		daban

Ustedes daban buenos regalos.
You used to give nice gifts.

Presente

Presente		INDICATIVO
	I give / I am giving	
	Irregular	
	Simple	Verbo
Yo	---	doy
Tú		das
Él/Ella/Usted		da
Nosotros/as		damos
Vosotros/as		dais
Éllos/Ellas/Ustedes		dan

Ustedes dan buenos regalos.
You give nice gifts.

Español Intermedio

Perfecto

Pluscuamperfecto		INDICATIVO
	I had given	
	Haber (Past Perfect) + Past Participle	
	Compueste	PP
Yo	había	dado
Tú	habías	
Él/Ella/Usted	había	
Nosotros/as	habíamos	
Vosotros/as	habíais	
Éllos/Ellas/Ustedes	habían	

Ustedes habían dado buenos regalos.
You had given nice gifts.

Presente Perfecto		INDICATIVO
	I have given	
	Haber (Present) + Past Participle	
	Compueste	PP
Yo	he	dado
Tú	has	
Él/Ella/Usted	ha	
Nosotros/as	hemos	
Vosotros/as	habéis	
Éllos/Ellas/Ustedes	han	

Ustedes han dado buenos regalos.
You have given nice gifts.

Progresivo

Imperfecto Progresivo		INDICATIVO
	I was giving	
	Estar (Imperfect) + Gerund	
	Compueste	Gerundio
Yo	estaba	dando
Tú	estabas	
Él/Ella/Usted	estaba	
Nosotros/as	estábamos	
Vosotros/as	estabais	
Éllos/Ellas/Ustedes	estaban	

Ustedes estaban dando buenos regalos.
You were giving nice gifts.

Presente Progresivo		INDICATIVO
	I am giving	
	Estar (Present) + Gerund	
	Compueste	Gerundio
Yo	estoy	dando
Tú	estás	
Él/Ella/Usted	está	
Nosotros/as	estamos	
Vosotros/as	estáis	
Éllos/Ellas/Ustedes	están	

Ustedes están dando buenos regalos.
You are giving nice gifts.

 joekazemi777@gmail.com

Futuro

Futuro — *INDICATIVO*

I will give

Irregular

	Simple	Verbo
Yo	---	daré
Tú		darás
Él/Ella/Usted		dará
Nosotros/as		daremos
Vosotros/as		daréis
Éllos/Ellas/Ustedes		darán

Ustedes darán buenos regalos.
You will give nice gifts.

Futuro Próximo — *INDICATIVO*

I am going to give

Ir (Present) + a + Infinitive

	Compueste	Infinitivo
Yo	voy a	dar
Tú	vas a	
Él/Ella/Usted	va a	
Nosotros/as	vamos a	
Vosotros/as	vais a	
Éllos/Ellas/Ustedes	van a	

Ustedes van a dar buenos regalos.
You are going to give nice gifts.

Futuro Perfecto — *INDICATIVO*

I will have given

Haber (Future) + Past Participle

	Compueste	PP
Yo	habré	dado
Tú	habrás	
Él/Ella/Usted	habrá	
Nosotros/as	habremos	
Vosotros/as	habréis	
Éllos/Ellas/Ustedes	habrán	

Ustedes habrán dado buenos regalos.
You will have given nice gifts.

Futuro Progresivo — *INDICATIVO*

I am going to be giving

Ir + a + Estar (Infinitive) + Gerund

	Compueste	Gerundio
Yo	voy a estar	dando
Tú	vas a estar	
Él/Ella/Usted	va a estar	
Nosotros/as	vamos a estar	
Vosotros/as	vais a estar	
Éllos/Ellas/Ustedes	van a estar	

Ustedes van a estar dando buenos regalos.
You are going to be giving nice gifts.

Condicional

Condicional — *CONDICIONAL*

I would give

Irregular

	Simple	Verbo
Yo	---	daría
Tú		darías
Él/Ella/Usted		dará
Nosotros/as		daríamos
Vosotros/as		daríais
Éllos/Ellas/Ustedes		darían

Ustedes darían buenos regalos.
You would give nice gifts.

Condicional Perfecto — *CONDICIONAL*

I would have given

Haber (Conditional) + Past Participle

	Compueste	PP
Yo	habría	dado
Tú	habrías	
Él/Ella/Usted	habría	
Nosotros/as	habríamos	
Vosotros/as	habríais	
Éllos/Ellas/Ustedes	habrían	

Ustedes habrían dado buenos regalos.
You would have given nice gifts.

Simple / Imperfecto — Español Principiante

Perfecto / Progresivo — Español Intermedio

13

salir — to leave

Español Principiante

Pasado

Simple

Pretérito		INDICATIVO
	I left	
	Irregular	
	Simple	Verbo
Yo	---	salí
Tú		saliste
Él/Ella/Usted		salió
Nosotros/as		salimos
Vosotros/as		salisteis
Éllos/Ellas/Ustedes		salieron
El autobús salió de la estación.		
The bus left the station.		

Imperfecto

Imperfecto		INDICATIVO
	I used to leave	
	Irregular	
	Simple	Verbo
Yo	---	salía
Tú		salías
Él/Ella/Usted		salía
Nosotros/as		salíamos
Vosotros/as		salíais
Éllos/Ellas/Ustedes		salían
El autobús salía de la estación.		
The bus used to leave the station.		

Presente

Presente		INDICATIVO
	I leave / I am leaving	
	Irregular	
	Simple	Verbo
Yo	---	salgo
Tú		sales
Él/Ella/Usted		sale
Nosotros/as		salimos
Vosotros/as		salís
Éllos/Ellas/Ustedes		salen
El autobús sale de la estación.		
The bus leaves the station.		

Español Intermedio

Perfecto

Pluscuamperfecto		INDICATIVO
	I had left	
	Haber (Past Perfect) + Past Participle	
	Compueste	PP
Yo	había	salido
Tú	habías	
Él/Ella/Usted	había	
Nosotros/as	habíamos	
Vosotros/as	habíais	
Éllos/Ellas/Ustedes	habían	
El autobús había salido de la estación.		
The bus had left the station.		

Presente Perfecto		INDICATIVO
	I have left	
	Haber (Present) + Past Participle	
	Compueste	PP
Yo	he	salido
Tú	has	
Él/Ella/Usted	ha	
Nosotros/as	hemos	
Vosotros/as	habéis	
Éllos/Ellas/Ustedes	han	
El autobús ha salido de la estación.		
The bus has left the station.		

Progresivo

Imperfecto Progresivo		INDICATIVO
	I was leaving	
	Estar (Imperfect) + Gerund	
	Compueste	Gerundio
Yo	estaba	saliendo
Tú	estabas	
Él/Ella/Usted	estaba	
Nosotros/as	estábamos	
Vosotros/as	estabais	
Éllos/Ellas/Ustedes	estaban	
El autobús estaba saliendo de la estación.		
The bus was leaving the station.		

Presente Progresivo		INDICATIVO
	I am leaving	
	Estar (Present) + Gerund	
	Compueste	Gerundio
Yo	estoy	saliendo
Tú	estás	
Él/Ella/Usted	está	
Nosotros/as	estamos	
Vosotros/as	estáis	
Éllos/Ellas/Ustedes	están	
El autobús está saliendo de la estación.		
The bus is leaving the station.		

 joekazemi777@gmail.com

Futuro

Futuro INDICATIVO

I will leave

Irregular

	Simple	Verbo
Yo	---	saldré
Tú		saldrás
Él/Ella/Usted		saldrá
Nosotros/as		saldremos
Vosotros/as		saldréis
Éllos/Ellas/Ustedes		saldrán

El autobús saldrá de la estación.
The bus will leave the station.

Futuro Próximo INDICATIVO

I am going to leave

Ir (Present) + a + Infinitive

	Compueste	Infinitivo
Yo	voy a	salir
Tú	vas a	
Él/Ella/Usted	va a	
Nosotros/as	vamos a	
Vosotros/as	vais a	
Éllos/Ellas/Ustedes	van a	

El autobús va a salir de la estación.
The bus is going to leave the station.

Futuro Perfecto INDICATIVO

I will have left

Haber (Future) + Past Participle

	Compueste	PP
Yo	habré	salido
Tú	habrás	
Él/Ella/Usted	habrá	
Nosotros/as	habremos	
Vosotros/as	habréis	
Éllos/Ellas/Ustedes	habrán	

El autobús habrá salido de la estación.
The bus will have left the station.

Futuro Progresivo INDICATIVO

I am going to be leaving

Ir + a + Estar (Infinitive) + Gerund

	Compueste	Gerundio
Yo	voy a estar	saliendo
Tú	vas a estar	
Él/Ella/Usted	va a estar	
Nosotros/as	vamos a estar	
Vosotros/as	vais a estar	
Éllos/Ellas/Ustedes	van a estar	

El autobús va a estar saliendo de la estación.
The bus is going to be leaving the station.

Condicional

Condicional CONDICIONAL

I would leave

Irregular

	Simple	Verbo
Yo	---	saldría
Tú		saldrías
Él/Ella/Usted		saldría
Nosotros/as		saldríamos
Vosotros/as		saldríais
Éllos/Ellas/Ustedes		saldrían

El autobús saldría de la estación.
The bus would leave the station.

Condicional Perfecto CONDICIONAL

I would have left

Haber (Conditional) + Past Participle

	Compueste	PP
Yo	habría	salido
Tú	habrías	
Él/Ella/Usted	habría	
Nosotros/as	habríamos	
Vosotros/as	habríais	
Éllos/Ellas/Ustedes	habrían	

El autobús habría salido de la estación.
The bus would have left the station.

Simple Imperfecto — Español Principiante

Perfecto Progresivo — Español Intermedio

14

pensar — to think / to plan

Español Principiante

Pasado — Simple

Pretérito		INDICATIVO
I thought		
Irregular		
	Simple	Verbo
Yo	---	pensé
Tú		pensaste
Él/Ella/Usted		pensó
Nosotros/as		pensamos
Vosotros/as		pensasteis
Éllos/Ellas/Ustedes		pensaron

Yo pensé en ti.
I thought of you.

Presente — Simple

Presente		INDICATIVO
I think / I am thinking		
Irregular		
	Simple	Verbo
Yo	---	pienso
Tú		piensas
Él/Ella/Usted		piensa
Nosotros/as		pensamos
Vosotros/as		pensáis
Éllos/Ellas/Ustedes		piensan

Yo pienso en ti.
I think of you.

Imperfecto

Imperfecto		INDICATIVO
I used to think		
Irregular		
	Simple	Verbo
Yo	---	pensaba
Tú		pensabas
Él/Ella/Usted		pensaba
Nosotros/as		pensábamos
Vosotros/as		pensabais
Éllos/Ellas/Ustedes		pensaban

Yo pensaba en ti.
I used to think of you.

Español Intermedio

Perfecto

Pluscuamperfecto		INDICATIVO
I had thought		
Haber (Past Perfect) + Past Participle		
	Compueste	PP
Yo	había	pensado
Tú	habías	
Él/Ella/Usted	había	
Nosotros/as	habíamos	
Vosotros/as	habíais	
Éllos/Ellas/Ustedes	habían	

Yo había pensado en ti.
I had thought of you.

Presente Perfecto		INDICATIVO
I have thought		
Haber (Present) + Past Participle		
	Compueste	PP
Yo	he	pensado
Tú	has	
Él/Ella/Usted	ha	
Nosotros/as	hemos	
Vosotros/as	habéis	
Éllos/Ellas/Ustedes	han	

Yo he pensado en ti.
I have thought of you.

Progresivo

Imperfecto Progresivo		INDICATIVO
I was thinking		
Estar (Imperfect) + Gerund		
	Compueste	Gerundio
Yo	estaba	pensando
Tú	estabas	
Él/Ella/Usted	estaba	
Nosotros/as	estábamos	
Vosotros/as	estabais	
Éllos/Ellas/Ustedes	estaban	

Yo estaba pensando en ti.
I was thinking of you.

Presente Progresivo		INDICATIVO
I am thinking		
Estar (Present) + Gerund		
	Compueste	Gerundio
Yo	estoy	pensando
Tú	estás	
Él/Ella/Usted	está	
Nosotros/as	estamos	
Vosotros/as	estáis	
Éllos/Ellas/Ustedes	están	

Yo estoy pensando en ti.
I am thinking of you.

 joekazemi777@gmail.com

Futuro

Futuro — *INDICATIVO*

I will think

Irregular

	Simple	Verbo
Yo	---	pensaré
Tú		pensarás
Él/Ella/Usted		pensará
Nosotros/as		pensaremos
Vosotros/as		pensaréis
Éllos/Ellas/Ustedes		pensarán

Yo pensaré en ti.
I will think of you.

Futuro Próximo — *INDICATIVO*

I am going to think

Ir (Present) + a + Infinitive

	Compueste	Infinitivo
Yo	voy a	pensar
Tú	vas a	
Él/Ella/Usted	va a	
Nosotros/as	vamos a	
Vosotros/as	vais a	
Éllos/Ellas/Ustedes	van a	

Yo voy a pensar en ti.
I am going to think of you.

Futuro Perfecto — *INDICATIVO*

I will have thought

Haber (Future) + Past Participle

	Compueste	PP
Yo	habré	pensado
Tú	habrás	
Él/Ella/Usted	habrá	
Nosotros/as	habremos	
Vosotros/as	habréis	
Éllos/Ellas/Ustedes	habrán	

Yo habré pensado en ti.
I will have thought of you.

Futuro Progresivo — *INDICATIVO*

I am going to be thinking

Ir + a + Estar (Infinitive) + Gerund

	Compueste	Gerundio
Yo	voy a estar	pensando
Tú	vas a estar	
Él/Ella/Usted	va a estar	
Nosotros/as	vamos a estar	
Vosotros/as	vais a estar	
Éllos/Ellas/Ustedes	van a estar	

Yo voy a estar pensando en ti.
I am going to be thinking of you.

Condicional

Condicional — CONDICIONAL

I would think

Irregular

	Simple	Verbo
Yo	---	pensaría
Tú		pensarías
Él/Ella/Usted		pensaría
Nosotros/as		pensaríamos
Vosotros/as		pensaríais
Éllos/Ellas/Ustedes		pensarían

Yo pensaré en ti.
I would think of you.

Condicional Perfecto — CONDICIONAL

I would have thought

Haber (Conditional) + Past Participle

	Compueste	PP
Yo	habría	pensado
Tú	habrías	
Él/Ella/Usted	habría	
Nosotros/as	habríamos	
Vosotros/as	habríais	
Éllos/Ellas/Ustedes	habrían	

Yo habría pensado en ti.
I would have thought of you.

Simple *Imperfecto* Español Principiante

Perfecto *Progresivo* Español Intermedio

15

traer — to bring / to carry

Español Principiante

Pasado — Simple

Pretérito		INDICATIVO
	I brought	
	Irregular	
	Simple	Verbo
Yo	---	traje
Tú		trajiste
Él/Ella/Usted		trajo
Nosotros/as		trajimos
Vosotros/as		trajisteis
Éllos/Ellas/Ustedes		trajeron

Nosotros trajimos las flores.
We brought flowers.

Presente — Simple

Presente		INDICATIVO
	I bring / I am bringing	
	Irregular	
	Simple	Verbo
Yo	---	traigo
Tú		traes
Él/Ella/Usted		trae
Nosotros/as		traemos
Vosotros/as		traéis
Éllos/Ellas/Ustedes		traen

Nosotros traemos las flores.
We bring flowers.

Pasado — Imperfecto

Imperfecto		INDICATIVO
	I used to bring	
	Irregular	
	Simple	Verbo
Yo	---	traía
Tú		traías
Él/Ella/Usted		traía
Nosotros/as		traíamos
Vosotros/as		traíais
Éllos/Ellas/Ustedes		traían

Nosotros trajimos las flores.
We used to bring flowers.

Español Intermedio

Perfecto

Pluscuamperfecto		INDICATIVO
	I had brought	
	Haber (Past Perfect) + Past Participle	
	Compueste	PP
Yo	había	traído
Tú	habías	
Él/Ella/Usted	había	
Nosotros/as	habíamos	
Vosotros/as	habíais	
Éllos/Ellas/Ustedes	habían	

Nosotros habíamos traído las flores.
We had brought flowers.

Presente Perfecto		INDICATIVO
	I have brought	
	Haber (Present) + Past Participle	
	Compueste	PP
Yo	he	traído
Tú	has	
Él/Ella/Usted	ha	
Nosotros/as	hemos	
Vosotros/as	habéis	
Éllos/Ellas/Ustedes	han	

Nosotros hemos traído las flores.
We have brought flowers.

Progresivo

Imperfecto Progresivo		INDICATIVO
	I was bringing	
	Estar (Imperfect) + Gerund	
	Compueste	Gerundio
Yo	estaba	trayendo
Tú	estabas	
Él/Ella/Usted	estaba	
Nosotros/as	estábamos	
Vosotros/as	estabais	
Éllos/Ellas/Ustedes	estaban	

Nosotros estábamos trayendo las flores.
We were bringing flowers.

Presente Progresivo		INDICATIVO
	I am bringing	
	Estar (Present) + Gerund	
	Compueste	Gerundio
Yo	estoy	trayendo
Tú	estás	
Él/Ella/Usted	está	
Nosotros/as	estamos	
Vosotros/as	estáis	
Éllos/Ellas/Ustedes	están	

Nosotros estamos trayendo las flores.
We are bringing flowers.

 joekazemi777@gmail.com

Futuro

Futuro — *INDICATIVO*

I will bring

Irregular

	Simple	Verbo
Yo	---	traeré
Tú		traerás
Él/Ella/Usted		traerá
Nosotros/as		traeremos
Vosotros/as		traeréis
Éllos/Ellas/Ustedes		traerán

Nosotros traeremos las flores.
We will bring flowers.

Futuro Próximo — *INDICATIVO*

I am going to bring

Ir (Present) + a + Infinitive

	Compueste	Infinitivo
Yo	voy a	traer
Tú	vas a	
Él/Ella/Usted	va a	
Nosotros/as	vamos a	
Vosotros/as	vais a	
Éllos/Ellas/Ustedes	van a	

Nosotros vamos a traer las flores.
We are going to bring flowers.

Futuro Perfecto — *INDICATIVO*

I will have brought

Haber (Future) + Past Participle

	Compueste	PP
Yo	habré	traído
Tú	habrás	
Él/Ella/Usted	habrá	
Nosotros/as	habremos	
Vosotros/as	habréis	
Éllos/Ellas/Ustedes	habrán	

Nosotros habremos traído las flores.
We will have brought flowers.

Futuro Progresivo — *INDICATIVO*

I am going to be bringing

Ir + a + Estar (Infinitive) + Gerund

	Compueste	Gerundio
Yo	voy a estar	trayendo
Tú	vas a estar	
Él/Ella/Usted	va a estar	
Nosotros/as	vamos a estar	
Vosotros/as	vais a estar	
Éllos/Ellas/Ustedes	van a estar	

Nosotros vamos a estar trayendo las flores.
We are going to be bringing flowers.

Condicional

Condicional — CONDICIONAL

I would bring

Irregular

	Simple	Verbo
Yo	---	traería
Tú		traerías
Él/Ella/Usted		traería
Nosotros/as		traeríamos
Vosotros/as		traeríais
Éllos/Ellas/Ustedes		traerían

Nosotros traeríamos las flores.
We would bring flowers.

Condicional Perfecto — CONDICIONAL

I would have brought

Haber (Conditional) + Past Participle

	Compueste	PP
Yo	habría	traído
Tú	habrías	
Él/Ella/Usted	habría	
Nosotros/as	habríamos	
Vosotros/as	habríais	
Éllos/Ellas/Ustedes	habrían	

Nosotros habríamos traído las flores.
We would have brought flowers.

Simple / *Imperfecto* — Español Principiante

Perfecto / *Progresivo* — Español Intermedio

16

abrir — to open

Español Principiante

Pasado / Presente

Simple

Pretérito — INDICATIVO

I opended

Irregular

	Simple	Verbo
Yo	---	abrí
Tú		abriste
Él/Ella/Usted		abrió
Nosotros/as		abrimos
Vosotros/as		abristeis
Éllos/Ellas/Ustedes		abrieron

La biblioteca pública abrió a las diez.
The public library opened at ten.

Presente — INDICATIVO

I open / I am opening

Irregular

	Simple	Verbo
Yo	---	abro
Tú		abres
Él/Ella/Usted		abre
Nosotros/as		abrimos
Vosotros/as		abrís
Éllos/Ellas/Ustedes		abren

La biblioteca pública abre a las diez.
The public library opens at ten.

Imperfecto

Imperfecto — INDICATIVO

I used to open

Irregular

	Simple	Verbo
Yo	---	abría
Tú		abrías
Él/Ella/Usted		abría
Nosotros/as		abríamos
Vosotros/as		abríais
Éllos/Ellas/Ustedes		abrían

La biblioteca pública abría a las diez.
The public library used to open at ten.

Español Intermedio

Perfecto

Pluscuamperfecto — INDICATIVO

I had opened

Haber (Past Perfect) + Past Participle

	Compueste	PP
Yo	había	abierto
Tú	habías	
Él/Ella/Usted	había	
Nosotros/as	habíamos	
Vosotros/as	habíais	
Éllos/Ellas/Ustedes	habían	

La biblioteca pública había abierto a las diez.
The public library had opened at ten.

Presente Perfecto — INDICATIVO

I have opened

Haber (Present) + Past Participle

	Compueste	PP
Yo	he	abierto
Tú	has	
Él/Ella/Usted	ha	
Nosotros/as	hemos	
Vosotros/as	habéis	
Éllos/Ellas/Ustedes	han	

La biblioteca pública ha abierto a las diez.
The public library has opened at ten.

Progresivo

Imperfecto Progresivo — INDICATIVO

I was opening

Estar (Imperfect) + Gerund

	Compueste	Gerundio
Yo	estaba	abriendo
Tú	estabas	
Él/Ella/Usted	estaba	
Nosotros/as	estábamos	
Vosotros/as	estabais	
Éllos/Ellas/Ustedes	estaban	

La biblioteca pública estaba abriendo a las diez.
The public library was opening at ten.

Presente Progresivo — INDICATIVO

I am opening

Estar (Present) + Gerund

	Compueste	Gerundio
Yo	estoy	abriendo
Tú	estás	
Él/Ella/Usted	está	
Nosotros/as	estamos	
Vosotros/as	estáis	
Éllos/Ellas/Ustedes	están	

La biblioteca pública está abriendo a las diez.
The public library is opening at ten.

 joekazemi777@gmail.com

Futuro

Futuro — INDICATIVO

I will open

Irregular

	Simple	Verbo
Yo	---	abriré
Tú		abrirás
Él/Ella/Usted		abrirá
Nosotros/as		abriremos
Vosotros/as		abriréis
Éllos/Ellas/Ustedes		abriréis

La biblioteca pública abrirá a las diez.
The public library will open at ten.

Futuro Próximo — INDICATIVO

I am going to open

Ir (Present) + a + Infinitive

	Compueste	Infinitivo
Yo	voy a	abrir
Tú	vas a	
Él/Ella/Usted	va a	
Nosotros/as	vamos a	
Vosotros/as	vais a	
Éllos/Ellas/Ustedes	van a	

La biblioteca pública va a abrir a las diez.
The public library is going to open at ten.

Futuro Perfecto — INDICATIVO

I will have opened

Haber (Future) + Past Participle

	Compueste	PP
Yo	habré	abierto
Tú	habrás	
Él/Ella/Usted	habrá	
Nosotros/as	habremos	
Vosotros/as	habréis	
Éllos/Ellas/Ustedes	habrán	

La biblioteca pública habrá abierto a las diez.
The public library will have opened at ten.

Futuro Progresivo — INDICATIVO

I am going to be opening

Ir + a + Estar (Infinitive) + Gerund

	Compueste	Gerundio
Yo	voy a estar	abriendo
Tú	vas a estar	
Él/Ella/Usted	va a estar	
Nosotros/as	vamos a estar	
Vosotros/as	vais a estar	
Éllos/Ellas/Ustedes	van a estar	

La biblioteca pública va a estar abriendo a las diez.
The public library is going to be opening at ten.

Condicional

Condicional — CONDICIONAL

I would open

Irregular

	Simple	Verbo
Yo	---	abriría
Tú		abrirías
Él/Ella/Usted		abriría
Nosotros/as		abriríamos
Vosotros/as		abriríais
Éllos/Ellas/Ustedes		abrirían

La biblioteca pública abriría a las diez.
The public library would open at ten.

Condicional Perfecto — CONDICIONAL

I would have opened

Haber (Conditional) + Past Participle

	Compueste	PP
Yo	habría	abierto
Tú	habrías	
Él/Ella/Usted	habría	
Nosotros/as	habríamos	
Vosotros/as	habríais	
Éllos/Ellas/Ustedes	habrían	

La biblioteca pública habría abierto a las diez.
The public library would have opened at ten.

17

jugar — to play

Español Principiante

Pasado — Presente

Simple

Pretérito		INDICATIVO
	I played	
	Irregular	
	Simple	Verbo
Yo	---	jugué
Tú		jugaste
Él/Ella/Usted		jugó
Nosotros/as		jugamos
Vosotros/as		jugasteis
Éllos/Ellas/Ustedes		jugaron

Éllos jugaron al fútbol en la playa.
They played soccer on the beach.

Presente		INDICATIVO
	I play / I am playing	
	Irregular	
	Simple	Verbo
Yo	---	juego
Tú		juegas
Él/Ella/Usted		juega
Nosotros/as		jugamos
Vosotros/as		jugáis
Éllos/Ellas/Ustedes		juegan

Éllos juegan al fútbol en la playa.
They play soccer on the beach.

Imperfecto

Imperfecto		INDICATIVO
	I used to play	
	Irregular	
	Simple	Verbo
Yo	---	jugaba
Tú		jugabas
Él/Ella/Usted		jugaba
Nosotros/as		jugábamos
Vosotros/as		jugabais
Éllos/Ellas/Ustedes		jugaban

Éllos jugaban al fútbol en la playa.
They used to play soccer on the beach.

Español Intermedio

Perfecto

Pluscuamperfecto		INDICATIVO
	I had played	
	Haber (Past Perfect) + Past Participle	
	Compueste	PP
Yo	había	jugado
Tú	habías	
Él/Ella/Usted	había	
Nosotros/as	habíamos	
Vosotros/as	habíais	
Éllos/Ellas/Ustedes	habían	

Éllos habían jugado al fútbol en la playa.
They had played soccer on the beach.

Presente Perfecto		INDICATIVO
	I have played	
	Haber (Present) + Past Participle	
	Compueste	PP
Yo	he	jugado
Tú	has	
Él/Ella/Usted	ha	
Nosotros/as	hemos	
Vosotros/as	habéis	
Éllos/Ellas/Ustedes	han	

Éllos han jugado al fútbol en la playa.
They have played soccer on the beach.

Progresivo

Imperfecto Progresivo		INDICATIVO
	I was playing	
	Estar (Imperfect) + Gerund	
	Compueste	Gerundio
Yo	estaba	jugando
Tú	estabas	
Él/Ella/Usted	estaba	
Nosotros/as	estábamos	
Vosotros/as	estabais	
Éllos/Ellas/Ustedes	estaban	

Éllos estaban jugando al fútbol en la playa.
They were playing soccer on the beach.

Presente Progresivo		INDICATIVO
	I am playing	
	Estar (Present) + Gerund	
	Compueste	Gerundio
Yo	estoy	jugando
Tú	estás	
Él/Ella/Usted	está	
Nosotros/as	estamos	
Vosotros/as	estáis	
Éllos/Ellas/Ustedes	están	

Éllos están jugando al fútbol en la playa.
They are playing soccer on the beach.

 joekazemi777@gmail.com

Futuro

Futuro *INDICATIVO*

I will play

Irregular

	Simple	Verbo
Yo	---	jugaré
Tú		jugarás
Él/Ella/Usted		jugará
Nosotros/as		jugaremos
Vosotros/as		jugaréis
Éllos/Ellas/Ustedes		jugarán

Éllos jugarán al fútbol en la playa.
They will play soccer on the beach.

Futuro Próximo *INDICATIVO*

I am going to play

Ir (Present) + a + Infinitive

	Compueste	Infinitivo
Yo	voy a	jugar
Tú	vas a	
Él/Ella/Usted	va a	
Nosotros/as	vamos a	
Vosotros/as	vais a	
Éllos/Ellas/Ustedes	van a	

Éllos van a jugar al fútbol en la playa.
They are going to play soccer on the beach.

Futuro Perfecto *INDICATIVO*

I will have played

Haber (Future) + Past Participle

	Compueste	PP
Yo	habré	jugado
Tú	habrás	
Él/Ella/Usted	habrá	
Nosotros/as	habremos	
Vosotros/as	habréis	
Éllos/Ellas/Ustedes	habrán	

Éllos habrán jugado al fútbol en la playa.
They will have played soccer on the beach.

Futuro Progresivo *INDICATIVO*

I am going to be playing

Ir + a + Estar (Infinitive) + Gerund

	Compueste	Gerundio
Yo	voy a estar	jugando
Tú	vas a estar	
Él/Ella/Usted	va a estar	
Nosotros/as	vamos a estar	
Vosotros/as	vais a estar	
Éllos/Ellas/Ustedes	van a estar	

Éllos van a estar jugando al fútbol en la playa.
They are going to be playing soccer on the beach.

Condicional

Condicional CONDICIONAL

I would play

Irregular

	Simple	Verbo
Yo	---	jugaría
Tú		jugarías
Él/Ella/Usted		jugaría
Nosotros/as		jugaríamos
Vosotros/as		jugaríais
Éllos/Ellas/Ustedes		jugarían

Éllos jugarían al fútbol en la playa.
They would play soccer on the beach.

Condicional Perfecto CONDICIONAL

I would have played

Haber (Conditional) + Past Participle

	Compueste	PP
Yo	habría	jugado
Tú	habrías	
Él/Ella/Usted	habría	
Nosotros/as	habríamos	
Vosotros/as	habríais	
Éllos/Ellas/Ustedes	habrían	

Éllos habrían jugado al fútbol en la playa.
They would have played soccer on the beach.

Simple *Imperfecto* *Español Principiante*

Perfecto *Progresivo* *Español Intermedio*

Blank

www.ingramcontent.com/pod-product-compliance
Ingram Content Group UK Ltd.
Pitfield, Milton Keynes, MK11 3LW, UK
UKHW051136260726
13967UKWH00010B/3089